This book belongs to:

_____

4

Sagittarius Daily Horoscope 2023

Sagittarius Daily Horoscope 2023

2023

JANUARY

M	T	W	T	F	S	S
						1
2	3	4	5	6	7	8
9	10	11	12	13	14	15
16	17	18	19	20	21	22
23	24	25	26	27	28	29
30	31					

FEBRUARY

M	T	W	T	F	S	S
		1	2	3	4	5
6	7	8	9	10	11	12
13	14	15	16	17	18	19
20	21	22	23	24	25	26
27	28					

MARCH

M	T	W	T	F	S	S
		1	2	3	4	5
6	7	8	9	10	11	12
13	14	15	16	17	18	19
20	21	22	23	24	25	26
27	28	29	30	31		

APRIL

M	T	W	T	F	S	S
					1	2
3	4	5	6	7	8	9
10	11	12	13	14	15	16
17	18	19	20	21	22	23
24	25	26	27	28	29	30

MAY

M	T	W	T	F	S	S
1	2	3	4	5	6	7
8	9	10	11	12	13	14
15	16	17	18	19	20	21
22	23	24	25	26	27	28
29	30	31				

JUNE

M	T	W	T	F	S	S
			1	2	3	4
5	6	7	8	9	10	11
12	13	14	15	16	17	18
19	20	21	22	23	24	25
26	27	28	29	30		

JULY

M	T	W	T	F	S	S
					1	2
3	4	5	6	7	8	9
10	11	12	13	14	15	16
17	18	19	20	21	22	23
24	25	26	27	28	29	30
31						

AUGUST

M	T	W	T	F	S	S
	1	2	3	4	5	6
7	8	9	10	11	12	13
14	15	16	17	18	19	20
21	22	23	24	25	26	27
28	29	30	31			

SEPTEMBER

M	T	W	T	F	S	S
				1	2	3
4	5	6	7	8	9	10
11	12	13	14	15	16	17
18	19	20	21	22	23	24
25	26	27	28	29	30	

OCTOBER

M	T	W	T	F	S	S
						1
2	3	4	5	6	7	8
9	10	11	12	13	14	15
16	17	18	19	20	21	22
23	24	25	26	27	28	29
30	31					

NOVEMBER

M	T	W	T	F	S	S
		1	2	3	4	5
6	7	8	9	10	11	12
13	14	15	16	17	18	19
20	21	22	23	24	25	26
27	28	29	30			

DECEMBER

M	T	W	T	F	S	S
				1	2	3
4	5	6	7	8	9	10
11	12	13	14	15	16	17
18	19	20	21	22	23	24
25	26	27	28	29	30	31

Eclipses

Hybrid Solar – April 20th

Penumbral Lunar – May 5th

Annular Solar – October 14th

Partial Lunar -October 28th

Equinoxes and Solstices

Spring - March 20th 21:25

Summer - June 21st 14:52

Fall – September 23rd 06:50

Winter – December 22nd 03:28

Mercury Retrogrades

December 29th, 2022 Capricorn - January 18th Capricorn

April 21st Taurus – May 15th Taurus

August 23rd Virgo – September 15th Virgo

December 13th Capricorn - January 2nd, 2024 Sagittarius

2023 FULL MOONS

Wolf Moon: January 6th, 23:09

Snow Moon: February 5th, 18:30

Worm Moon March 7th, 12:40

Pink Moon: April 6th, 4:37

Flower Moon: May 5th, 17:34

Strawberry Moon: June 4th, 3:42

Buck Moon: July 3rd, 11:40

Sturgeon Moon: August 1st, 18:32

Blue Moon: August 31st, 1:36

Corn, Harvest Moon: September 29th, 9:58

Hunters Moon: October 28th, 20:23

Beaver Moon: November 27th, 9:16

Cold Moon: December 27th, 0:34

2023 INGRESSES

Mars Ingresses

Mar 25, 2023, 11:36	Mars enters Cancer
May 20, 2023, 15:24	Mars enters Leo
Jul 10, 2023, 11:34	Mars enters Virgo
Aug 27, 2023, 13:15	Mars enters Libra
Oct 12, 2023, 3:39	Mars enters Scorpio
Nov 24, 2023, 10:10	Mars enters Sagittarius

Venus Ingresses

Jan 3, 2023, 2:06	Venus enters Aquarius
Jan 27, 2023, 2:29	Venus enters Pisces
Feb 20, 2023, 7:52	Venus enters Aries
Mar 16, 2023, 22:31	Venus enters Taurus
Apr 11, 2023, 4:43	Venus enters Gemini
May 7, 2023, 14:20	Venus enters Cancer
Jun 5, 2023, 13:42	Venus enters Leo
Oct 9, 2023, 1:06	Venus enters Virgo
Nov 8, 2023, 9:27	Venus enters Libra
Dec 4, 2023, 18:48	Venus enters Scorpio
Dec 29, 2023, 20:21	Venus enters Sagittarius

Mercury Ingresses

Feb 11, 2023, 11:22	Mercury enters Aquarius
Mar 2, 2023, 22:49	Mercury enters Pisces
Mar 19, 2023, 04:22	Mercury enters Aries
Apr 3, 2023, 16:20	Mercury enters Taurus
Jun 11, 2023, 10:24	Mercury enters Gemini
Jun 27, 2023, 0:22	Mercury enters Cancer
Jul 11, 2023, 4:09	Mercury enters Leo
Jul 28, 2023, 21:29	Mercury enters Virgo
Oct 5, 2023, 0:06	Mercury enters Libra
Oct 22, 2023, 6:46	Mercury enters Scorpio
Nov 10, 2023, 6:22	Mercury enters Sagittarius
Dec 1, 2023, 14:29	Mercury enters Capricorn

Slower Moving Ingresses

Mar 7, 2023, 13:03	Saturn enters Pisces
Mar 23, 2023, 8:42	Pluto enters Aquarius
May 16, 2023, 17:01	Jupiter enters Taurus

The Moon Phases

- New Moon (Dark Moon)
- Waxing Crescent Moon
- First Quarter Moon
- Waxing Gibbous Moon
- Full Moon
- Waning Gibbous (Disseminating) Moon
- Third (Last/Reconciling) Quarter Moon
- Waning Crescent (Balsamic) Moon

● New Moon (Dark Moon)

The New Moon reveals what hides beyond the realm of everyday circumstances. It creates space to focus on contemplation and the gathering of wisdom. It is the beginning of the moon cycles. It is a time for plotting your course and planning for the future. It does let you unearth new possibilities when you tap into the wisdom of what is flying under the radar. You can embrace positivity, change, and adaptability. Harness the New Moon's power to set the stage for developing your trailblazing ideas. It is a Moon phase for hatching plans for nurturing ideas. Creativity is quickening; thoughts are flexible and innovative. Epiphanies are prevalent during this time.

● Waxing Crescent Moon

It is the Moon's first step forward on her journey towards fullness. Change is in the air, it can feel challenging to see the path ahead, yet something is tempting you forward. Excitement and inspiration are in the air. It epitomizes a willingness to be open to change and grow your world. This Moon often brings surprises, good news, seed money, and secret information. This Moon brings opportunities that are a catalyst for change. It tempts the debut of wild ideas and goals. It catapults you towards growth and often brings a breakthrough that sweeps in and demands your attention. Changes in the air inspiration weave the threads of manifestation around your awareness.

◑ First Quarter Moon

The First Quarter Moon is when exactly half of the Moon is shining. It signifies that action is ready to be taken. You face a crossroads; decisive action clears the path. You cut through indecisiveness and make your way forward. There is a sense of something growing during this phase. Your creativity nourishes the seeds you planted. As you reflect on this journey, you draw equilibrium and balance the First Quarter Moon's energy before tipping the scales in your favor. You feel a sense of accomplishment of having made progress on your journey, yet, there is still a long way to go. Pause, contemplate the path ahead, and nurture your sense of perseverance and grit, as things have a ways to go.

◔ Waxing Gibbous Moon

Your plans are growing; the devil is in the detail; a meticulous approach lets you achieve the highest result. You may find a boost arrives and gives a shot of can-do energy. It connects you with new information about the path ahead. The Moon is growing, as is your creativity, inspiration, and focus. It is also a time of essential adjustments, streamlining, evaluating goals, and plotting your course towards the final destination. Success is within reach; a final push will get you through. The wind is beneath your wings, a conclusion within reach, and you have the tools at your disposal to achieve your vision.

Full Moon

The Full Moon is when you often reach a successful conclusion. It does bring a bounty that adds to your harvest. Something unexpected often unfolds that transforms your experience. It catches you by surprise, a breath of fresh air; it is a magical time that lets you appreciate what your work has achieved. It is time for communication and sharing thoughts and ideas. It often brings a revelation eliminating new information. The path clears, and you release doubt, anxiety, and tension. It is a therapeutic and healing time that lets you release old energy positively and supportively.

Waning Gibbous (Disseminating) Moon

The Waning gibbous Moon is perfect for release; it allows you to cut away from areas that hold back true potential. You may feel drained as you have worked hard, journeyed long, and are now creating space to return and complete the cycle. It does see tools arrive to support and nourish your spirit. Creating space to channel your energy effectively and cutting away outworn regions creates an environment that lets your ideas and efforts bloom. It is a healing time, a time of acceptance that things move forward towards completing a cycle. This casting off the outworn debris that accumulates over the lunar month is a vital cleansing that clears space and resolves complex emotions that may cling to your energy if not addressed.

Third (Last/Reconciling) Quarter Moon

This Moon is about stabilizing your foundations. There is uncertainty shifting sands; as change surrounds your life, take time to be mindful of drawing balance into your world. It is the perfect time to reconnect with simple past times and hobbies. Securing and tethering your energy does build a stable foundation from which to grow your world. It is time to take stock and balance areas of your life. Consolidating your power by nurturing your inner child lets you embrace a chapter to focus on the areas that bring you joy. It is not time to advance or acquire new goals. The restful phase speaks of simple pastimes that nurture your spirit.

Waning Crescent (Balsamic) Moon

The Waning Crescent Moon completes the cycle; this Moon finishes the set. It lets you tie up loose ends, finish the finer details, and create space for new inspiration to flow into your world once the cycle begins. The word balsamic speaks of healing and attending to areas that feel raw or sensitive. It is a mystical phase that reconnects you to the process of life. As the Moon dies away, you can move away from areas that feel best left behind. Focusing on healing, meditation, self-care, and nurturing one's spirit is essential during this Moon phase.

The Full Moon: How it can affect your star sign

The Full Moon shines a light on areas that seek adjustment or healing in your life.

The Full Moon is a time to bring awareness into your spirit of the areas that seek resolution or adjustment. Over time, the past can create emotional blockages in your life. The Full Moon forms a sacred space to process sensitive emotions and release the past's hold on your spirit.

This lunar vibration brings awareness to your spirit of how your emotions affect your daily life. When the Moon is complete, your emotional awareness magnifies, and you feel things more intensely in your everyday life.

The Full Moon brings a chance to go over the inner terrain and connect with your intuition. She shines a light on areas that hold the most significant meaning in your life. This effect has a powerful impact on creativity, planning, and future life direction. Listening to your gut instincts helps you strip away from areas that only cloud judgment and muddy your awareness.

Sagittarius: The Full Moon washes away outworn areas; it cleanses your spirit and leaves you feeling reinvigorated. It brings clarity that helps you be impeccable with judging others and their motives. Pay close attention to what surfaces under the Full Moon. Expect insights and hidden information to appear. Resolving sensitive emotions promotes stability that gets you back on track after your Full Moon healing.

I use the 24-hour clock/military time.
Time set to Coordinated Universal Time Zone (UT±0)

I've noted Meteor Showers on the date they peak.

January

Sun	Mon	Tue	Wed	Thu	Fri	Sat
1	2	3	4	5	6	7
8	9	10	11	12	13	14
15	16	17	18	19	20	21
22	23	24	25	26	27	28
29	30	31				

New Moon

WOLF MOON

30 Friday

Life heats up with new potential soon. With an invitation and lengthy conversations, see your social life turns the corner and head to a happy chapter. Support swirling around your life gives you the green light to network and connect with friends. A social path blossoms under a productive sky. It is a time that nurtures well-being as it draws new possibilities into your world.

31 Saturday

Information arrives soon that stirs up new potential. It gives you a chance to build strong foundations. It does bring a transition that helps you break through to a lucky chapter. It draws more stability into your world, heightening the sense of well-being and harmony. You are ready to nurture a new area; as you direct your energy towards growing your world, you discover an opportunity to learn and prosper.

1 Sunday ~ New Year's Day, Venus conjunct Pluto 5:24

Venus, the ruler of love, offers an abundant landscape when conjunct with Pluto. The energy of transformation surrounds your life, enabling you to advance your romantic life. It brings the potential to cultivate romance and magic in your world. You attract the abundance that supports and sustains you as you get busy and explore this pathway forward for your personal life.

2 Monday ~ Mercury sextile Neptune 6:53

This sextile attracts free-flowing and creative ideas that help you place the cherry on this year's plans and aspirations. It draws an abundant landscape filled with happiness and harmony as a strong emphasis on goals around your life draw stability and joy. It opens new possibilities for your life and brings a journey worth savoring. Information arrives that grows your experience by allowing you to make good headway around some of your larger goals.

3 Tuesday ~ Venus ingress Aquarius 2:06, Quadrantids Meteors runs Jan 1st – 5th

Perseverance and determination help you juggle life and maintain various projects while keeping your eye on new possibilities. If you feel stuck or restricted, remember to get those balls in the air and start shifting your energy forward. Setting aspirations and goals activate your power and primes your creativity. It brings new ideas that help cut away from areas that didn't bear fruit.

4 Wednesday ~ Venus sextile Jupiter 9:07

This sextile attracts warm and abundant energy into your social life. A dash of luck and good fortune combined with enriching conversations improve social bonds in your life. Life lights up when you discover new possibilities that kickstart growth in your life. It marks a time that enhances circumstances, increasing the happiness in your world. It brings thoughtful ideas and connects with people who surround your life.

5 Thursday ~ Sun trine Uranus 16:43

This Sun trine Uranus transit brings positive change and excitement into your world. You enter a stirring chapter that lifts the lid on rising options for your life. You soon find the motivation to put something that has been on the back burner of your life front and center in your world. Exploring and launching your abilities into a unique area nurtures stable foundations in your life. A situation you cultivate blossoms into a dynamic path forward.

6 Friday ~ Wolf Full Moon in Cancer 23:09

You can use this Full Moon to release the turbulence in your life. You soon find stable foundations which ground your spirit in a new area of interest. Re-evaluating the path ahead helps you ascertain the right way forward. You enter a more stable phase that brings a passageway towards a brighter future. It lets you release any restrictive patterns and advance towards more critical goals in your life.

7 Saturday ~ Sun Conjunct Mercury 12:56

This conjunct bodes well for communication. Rising prospects draw insightful conversations that stimulate creativity and problem-solving mental energy. It lights up a pathway that offers improvement as it takes you toward an exciting destination. You can feel confident when you cast your net of dreams comprehensively, enabling you to come up with the proper catch. Being open and willing to a new realm of options draws a pleasing result for your life.

8 Sunday ~ Mercury trine Uranus 23:22

Mercury forming a trine with Uranus brings flashes of insight; expect an epiphany as brilliance surrounds your thought processes today. Pushing back the barriers and exploring a wider world of possibilities reveals an opportunity that broadens your horizons. A positive trend brings a stable foundation that lets you make notable tracks on advancing your goals to the next level.

9 Monday ~ Venus trine Mars 15:21

This week, Venus trine Mars raises your energy and brings a vibrant passion for life. Your willingness to push boundaries back is fundamental in revealing the highest potential possible. It gets a journey worth developing as it grows your abilities in critical areas that extend your reach into new options. It brings a journey that advances your skills and moves your life towards a unique assignment.

10 Tuesday

You may be questioning the path ahead. Feeling restless or disconnected is an invitation to broaden your horizons. Rest assured, you will find a direction to channel your wild and rebellious energy into, transforming it into a functional area where you can grow. Experimenting and exploring pathways bring ideal spice and an experimental flavor to the mix of potential. It is a perfect time for setting intentions and directing your purpose towards developing your goals.

11 Wednesday

An emphasis on friendship reveals a secret. It shines a light on companionship and developing a bond that offers room to grow into a meaningful situation. Being open to change broadens your perception and brings a new possibility to light. Plenty of good energy flows easily and naturally around your social life; it brings a happy and optimistic chapter ahead. Abundance flourishes as you reveal information that brings a stir of excitement.

12 Thursday ~ Mars turns direct at 20:54

With the planet Mars moving forward, your energy, passion, and drive return to full force. News arrives, tinged with the currency of change. It imbues a sense of purpose as it offers a more driven chapter of growth in your life. Something curious on offer tides you over nicely as it improves the foundations of your world. It gives you a stable basis; inspiration rises, thinking about future possibilities.

13 Friday ~ Sun sextile Neptune 14:11

Resources and support help you get busy manifesting your vision. A richly creative process is the crux of developing your abilities and nurturing your talents. You soon get active on a trail that inspires growth. It lets you remove any elements that are no longer relevant and head towards a journey that offers expansion and happiness. As you continue to attract positive results, the essence of manifestation surrounds your life.

14 Saturday

News arrives that kicks off a chapter of improving your life. It triggers an active phase of developing new goals and getting involved in the broader world of potential outside of your front door. You create a grounded and stable environment from which to grow your dreams. It brings a time of connecting with friends and mingling with people who inspire growth and progress in your world.

15 Sunday ~ Venus square Uranus 1:21, Last Quarter Moon in Libra 2:12

A Venus Uranus square creates a need to balance and harmonize interpersonal bonds while honoring your need for freedom and expression. Life brings new people into your life, shining a light on companionship. It brings a busy time for socializing, and this pairs well with your future goals. It opens a path towards a trailblazing time of expanding your life as you become involved with your broader community.

16 Monday ~ Martin Luther King Day

You soon enter a time for planning your future goals. Mapping your strategy is instrumental in setting your aspirations for this year. Growth and learning ahead create a strong foundation that nurtures your abilities. It brings a fresh start that helps you make a proper choice regarding your future. It brings an environment that is productive, lively, and active. As you advance outwardly, you soon make waves in an area that captures your interest.

17 Tuesday

New possibilities ahead light the fire in your belly. It sparks a journey that flings outworn energy to the curb. Confidence rises, leading the way towards developing a new endeavor. Working with your talents shines on your abilities and creates a stable basis for building your dreams. A clue ahead reveals an option that blossoms into a journey worth growing. It brings a time of dynamic activity that offers steady growth.

18 Wednesday ~ Mercury turns direct at 13:12

Mercury is the messenger planet of communication, collaboration, and creative expression. Life becomes more manageable and flows more easily during Mercury's direct phase. Improving circumstances is a unique theme that resonates strongly during growth and progress. Life becomes an upswing when you receive news that offers a social opportunity. Mingling and networking see life bubbling along and heading towards smoother sailing.

19 Thursday

Tearing down the barriers that prevent progress brings new possibilities into your life. It brings some exciting changes that let you move in a new direction. It offers improvement, strategy, and planning. Life picks up momentum; you thrive on new challenges and options in this active and dynamic landscape. Finding an outlet for excess energy lets you channel your talents into a valuable area.

20 Friday ~ Sun ingress Aquarius 8:26

Rebellious and untamed energy draw expansion and freedom. It does drive your motivation, and this inspires change and growth. Something new and exciting tempts you forward. It brings an impressive time of pushing back limitations and barriers to reaching your chosen destination. The wildness in your spirit brings results. It releases pressure and provides you with an enterprising path forward.

21 Saturday ~ New Moon in Aquarius 20:54

You face a crossroads, and this New Moon brings change. It does draw a reflective and introspective chapter as you contemplate the path ahead. You make a decision that brings a turning point. It liberates the tension and attracts abundance and social support. It does trigger a new chapter in your social life that draws the opportunity to nurture a bond. It brings a path that tempts you forward and enriches your life.

22 Sunday ~ Venus conjunct Saturn 22:12, Uranus turns direct 23:23
Chinese New Year (Rabbit)

The Chinese New Year heralds good luck and fortune. Rabbits are a symbol of growth and fertility. Ideas planted in fertile terrain will get a chance to blossom and grow. It brings the opportunity to work with your abilities and deepen your talents in an area that feels good for your soul. Indeed, nurturing well-being and happiness chart a course upward and onward.

23 Monday

A new chapter brings an original and creative journey. It paves the way forward for a productive time of learning a new area. Your willingness to open the door to new opportunities draws dividends. A lead emerges that provides a compelling journey of growing the path ahead. It launches your skills into an area that seeks expression, bringing tangible results as a prominent area comes calling.

24 Tuesday

A new option helps you move towards growth with a plan in place. It brings a shift forward that offers to advance your skills and grow your abilities. It brings a venture that harnesses the essence of manifestation. You settle into a productive groove that holds fantastic appeal for your life. Imagination and creativity run wild, drawing a journey of growth and evolution. It stirs the pot of possibility.

25 Wednesday ~ Sun sextile Jupiter 1:30

In sextile with Jupiter, the Sun attracts a restless vibe that has you yearning to expand your life outwardly. Good fortune lights a shimmering path forward that makes you eager to embark on a new journey. It offers vast horizons, and sharing with others draws well-being and harmony into your surroundings. Opportunity comes knocking when information catches your attention. It allows you to take the reins and move toward an enterprising chapter of growth.

26 Thursday

Spending time with your circle becomes a gateway from which you grow your world. News is afoot, bringing an invitation to mingle and taking you towards a happy chapter ahead. Being open to new possibilities draws positive energy, wiping the slate clean. It helps you begin a new chapter in your life. The path forward brings new opportunities which weave magic around your life.

27 Friday ~ Venus ingress Pisces 2:29

Being open to new possibilities helps create a gateway towards growing the potential possible in your world. You ride a wave of hopeful energy as you get back to basics. Your willingness to be open to new people brings golden moments overhead. It allows you to reinvent yourself and bring light energy into your life. Pouring your energy into developing social bonds brings a pleasing result.

28 Saturday ~ First Quarter Moon in Taurus 15:19

You open a social aspect that attracts lively companions. It leads to a busy time supporting a stable growth phase in your life. Sharing thoughts and ideas with friends draw a strong foundation that offers a pleasing result. It heightens security and brings opportunities to collaborate and develop new projects. You soon awaken to an influx of creative inspiration which becomes the gateway from which you grow your life outwardly.

29 Sunday

It is a time when you see improvement flowing into your world. It brings a social patch that connects you with someone who inspires your mind. It brings happy developments as life moves forward toward new opportunities. Nurturing your social life draws dividends. It gets personal growth and takes you towards an expressive, joyful, and abundant environment. Building stable foundations plant the right seeds.

February

Sun	Mon	Tue	Wed	Thu	Fri	Sat
			1	2	3	4
5	6	7	8	9	10	11
12	13	14	15	16	17	18
19	20	21	22	23	24	25
26	27	28				

NEW MOON

SNOW MOON

30 Monday ~ Sun trine Mars 1:45, Mercury trine Uranus 2:17
Mercury at Greatest Eastern Elongation: 25.0°W

Your unique gifts and creativity reveal a path that advances your abilities. It does bring an enterprising chapter of growing your situation through taking side journeys that light up your inspiration. Extra opportunities are opening soon that open the gates to a busy time. It brings an initiative that offers advancement. An organized approach provides a winning strategy.

31 Tuesday

A new option makes an entrance, getting a lead ripe for growth. Staying open to new possibilities, people, and resources, feed your creativity with new potential. Exciting changes are coming up that draw abundance. You spend time with kindred spirit spirits and enjoy creating space to share thoughts and ideas with others. You can cast your net wide as options emerge that spark your curiosity.

1 Wednesday ~ Imbolc

Your efforts to improve your circumstances bear fruit. It underscores a willingness to be flexible and adapt to change. More security on the home front releases tension and gives you a new page of potential. Releasing anxiety and flicking the stress to the far corners of your mind draws a vital benefit. It lets you see the abundance currently swirling around your life's periphery. New information breezes into your life and offers a lighter, happier phase.

2 Thursday~ Groundhog Day

It is the perfect time to plan, project, brainstorm, and gently use your creativity to find innovative solutions. If you are being held back in one area, move in a direction that gives you the green light. Prosperity is on the rise; a celebration ahead highlights a sense of optimism and abundance ready to flow through your life. You can focus on foundations and prepare to move forward. Indeed, options are looming that provide a path worth growing.

3 Friday

You approach a time of inspired possibilities that puts you in the mood to socialize. It brings optimistic energy that bolsters your spirit and provides a new chapter of potential. It gives you the green light to connect with your broader social environment. As you shift towards expansion, you engage with a refreshing world of options. It is a happy and beneficial time that draws harmony and joy.

4 Saturday ~ Sun square Uranus 2:50

This positive square offers rising creativity that cultivates a new approach. Something special is brewing in the background of your life. It brings developments that sow the seeds to nurture a dream. News arrives that brings a stroke of good fortune and expansion into your world. Being proactive lets, you unearth curious opportunities suitable for progression. You land in a landscape ready to blossom into a meaningful journey forward.

5 Sunday ~ Venus square Mars 3:28, Snow Full Moon in Leo 18:30

This square can cause challenges as a difference of opinion fosters tension and conflict. Flexibility, understanding, and adaptability will help harmonize bonds and limit the disruption caused by Venus facing Mars at a harsh angle. Being willing to compromise will improve the foundations and limit the disruption in your life. The Full Moon in Leo offers a therapeutic influence that links with a heart-centered time of healing the past.

6 Monday ~ Mercury sextile Neptune 18:27

Rational thinking and dreams align in this sextile. You see rising creativity and analytical thinking promoting epiphanies that count. This cosmic alignment helps your dreams become a reality as structured backing behind your vision offers tangible results. Information arrives that grows your experience by allowing you to make good headway around some of your larger goals. Planning, strategizing and exploring leads open a winning trajectory.

7 Tuesday

Beautiful changes ahead bring a positive sign that improvement is looming. It helps you turn a corner and head towards greener pastures as curious changes shift your focus to developing a unique journey forward. Setting intentions and aspirations helps nurture the essence of manifestation around your life. New possibilities draw a surge of optimism that brings a chance to advance skills. It translates to a fresh start, offering improved growth and excellent stability.

8 Wednesday ~ Venus sextile Uranus 5:28

Spontaneity, fun, and fresh adventures rule your social life with this engaging sextile. You make great tracks on developing your social life as it gets a friendly and lively environment. It draws new energy that reveals closer friendships and companions. A significant shift ahead takes you towards a happy chapter that nurtures well-being. Thoughtful conversations buoy your spirit. It brings good vibrations that nourish and renew your foundations.

9 Thursday

You discover a unique vantage point that brings a broader overview of your life. Gaining insight into the path ahead brings new avenues of growth that offer more excellent stability in your life. It lights an enchanting way forward that sees creativity coursing through your choices and decisions ahead. It brings a time of using your talents to forge an enterprising trail towards the development of dreams.

10 Friday ~ Mercury conjunct Pluto 17:16

Today's conjunct between Mercury and Pluto offers intense curiosity to delve a little deeper. Changes ahead enable you to cultivate magic and possibility. Many new options help you turn a corner and grow life in a new direction. Creativity and inspiration surge in your world as you hone in on a higher sense of purpose. The energy of manifestation blends with your aspirations to bring a vibrant landscape of potential.

11 Saturday ~ Mercury ingress Aquarius 11:22

The energy of manifestation blends with your aspirations to bring a vibrant landscape of potential. It brings grounded foundations that nurture well-being and happiness. It gets a chance to reinvent your abilities and grow your talents in a unique area of interest. Being open to the possibilities lets you channel your restless energy into an avenue that draws rising prospects into your life.

12 Sunday

Change surrounds your world and soon brings the type of forwarding progress you have been seeking. It offers a chance to deepen a friendship as it shines a light on your personal goals. It fuels an exciting chapter of social engagement that leads to expanding horizons. It brings motivation, creativity, and growth to the forefront of your life. It opens a new page that lets you feel optimistic about prospects.

13 Monday ~ Last Quarter Moon in Scorpio 16:01

You soon enter a busy time that expands life into new areas. It offers a creative and abundant time that grows your talents and nurtures your dreams. It brings a purposeful push towards learning and advancement that cracks the code to a brighter chapter. It offers a shift forward that brings a lovely boost as it highlights unique options that open the path toward growth. The wheels are soon in motion, bringing a dynamic and abundant landscape into focus.

14 Tuesday ~ Valentine's Day

Events on the horizon trigger a time of romantic expansion. You gain insight into your dreams and aspirations as you nurture this potential. It is a time of adventure ahead that fuels your imagination with inspiration and excitement. Being open to change lets you explore new vistas of possibility. It takes you beyond your current environment and to a time of romance and magic for your personal life.

15 Wednesday ~ Venus conjunct Neptune 12:25

Venus joins forces with Neptune, and your love life takes on a dreamy quality as you engage in fanciful thoughts and contemplation. The desire moves into unlimited imagination as you think about the future, intending to nurture romance in your life. Events on the horizon trigger growth in your life. It allows you to open a unique path filled with possibilities. It is a time that brings both manifestations and transitions your way.

16 Thursday ~ Saturn conjunct Sun 16:48

Saturn connects with the Sun to blaze a trail towards developing your goals. Getting serious about limiting distractions and cultivating discipline, concentration, and order will help you nail progress in your working life. Gaining traction on improving security in your world will bring a valuable sense of achievement and accomplishment to your door.

17 Friday

You discover a treasure trove of possibilities that keeps the fires of potential burning. It unlocks a pathway of growth and rising prospects which help smooth out any bumpy patches. Developing your talents nurtures growth, and this progress enables you to climb the ladder towards a successful outcome. Impending news ahead brings a forward-facing environment that launches an endeavor close to your heart.

18 Saturday ~ Mercury sextile Jupiter 2:13, Sun ingress Pisces 22:30

The Mercury Jupiter aspect creates harmony between both planets. It sparks rising curiosity, questioning, and fresh ideas as an exciting journey ahead fill in the blanks. It starts a new trend in your life that migrates away from difficulties as you embark on making the most of an influx of options that grow your abilities. Moving in alignment with the person you are becoming nurtures inspiration and passion.

19 Sunday ~ Venus sextile Pluto 17:04

Today's Venus and Pluto alignment offers depth and insight into your thought processes. It helps you dig a little deeper and discover what drives your passion. Thinking about the areas that hold the most significant meaning in your life can be helpful on many levels. It weeds out the deals that are no longer a good fit for your life by letting you see the most meaningful aspects of your world.

20 Monday ~ Presidents' Day. New Moon in Pisces 7:08, Venus ingress Aries 7:52

A reconnection is coming that offers a closer friendship with someone who has drifted from your social circle over recent months. This person hopes to build a closer bond and open pathways of communication. It brings a shift forward that fuels an exciting chapter in your social life. It does set the stage for an exciting and lively time of new adventures with someone who seeks to build a brighter future with you.

21 Tuesday ~ Shrove Tuesday (Mardi Gras), Mercury square Uranus 22:22

Original thinking, creative brainstorming, and insightful epiphanies are the order of the day as Mercury squares off against Uranus today. It ignites fresh ideas that kick off a time of thoughtful discussions. Greener pastures beckon as you launch life forward. It places you in a solid position to improve your circumstances by following your internal compass. Ideas blossom when shared and blend beautifully with others who share insights.

22 Wednesday ~ Ash Wednesday, Lent Begins, Mercury trine Mars 20:14

A Mercury trine Mars aspect attracts a restless vibe. This cosmic alignment leaves you feeling spontaneous and ready for new adventures today. Many new options are coming into your world soon. Being open and receptive to change helps you discover leads that advance life forward. It brings the opportunity to deepen your artistic talents and share your gifts with a broader audience. Creative expression is at the crux of an enterprising time ahead.

23 Thursday

You may find priorities shift as you build foundations that expand life outwardly. It illuminates a path of growth, learning, and potential. It helps create a solid base to grow your vision for future development. A surge of inspiring options takes your talents to the next level. It brings a refreshing change of pace that dissolves restrictive patterns and creates space to use your abilities wisely.

24 Friday

You feel a strong pull towards expanding your social life. It does light a visionary quest that sparks new adventures with kindred spirits. Your life fills with invitations to social events and opportunities to mingle. It lets you dream big and develop personal bonds that support and nurture your dreams. It brings your life to the next level. It does allow you to carve out time to expand your horizons and bring possibilities to life in your social life.

25 Saturday

Getting in touch with your dreams sets the stage for a new chapter. It brings deeper self-awareness and lets you tap into your deeper needs and desires. You are ready to nurture a new journey, and a wave of information arrives to tempt you towards growth. It brings changes that draw growth and abundance. It brings a broad idea of what is possible in your situation, which sweeps in new possibilities.

26 Sunday

You find you can make headway on your vision and achieve a pleasing result for your life. It lets you pass the threshold towards a lighter, happier landscape. You are entering a transitional time. It does bring change, and it is imperative to focus on your home environment. It brings stability to your foundations, giving you a chance to build a fruitful and robust basis from which to chart your next set of goals.

MARCH

Sun	Mon	Tue	Wed	Thu	Fri	Sat
			1	2	3	4
5	6	7	8	9	10	11
12	13	14	15	16	17	18
19	20	21	22	23	24	25
26	27	28	29	30	31	

NEW MOON

WORM MOON

27 Monday ~ First Quarter Moon in Gemini 8:06

A bright, breezy wind of refreshing potential puts a lighter influence into your sails. It helps you embark on a voyage that reshuffles the decks of fate. The journey ahead glimmers with possibilities, bringing rising prospects that facilitate advancement. New leads emerge which have you thinking about the options. It brings a time of developing areas that motivate change. Life takes on a rosy hue when your willingness to explore new possibilities brings rewards.

28 Tuesday

You unveil a new option soon that has you contemplating the path ahead in a new light. It places a focus on your long-term goals and dreams. It highlights a path of discovery that offers new options and possibilities. It fuels your ambition and shows the progress that tempts you towards change. Focusing on strategy and planning for unexpected contingencies lets you create a stable basis for plotting a course forward towards your vision.

1 Wednesday

You spot an opportunity when you move out of your usual routine. It does bring a catalyst for change that is therapeutic for your spirit. It helps heal old areas that trigger sensitive emotions. It sets the stage for a path of happiness to enter your world. It begins a time of planning and projecting your dreams and aspirations, allowing them to take shape. It brings a revamp that sweeps in new potential.

2 Thursday ~ Venus conjunct Jupiter 17:35, Mercury conjunct Saturn 14:34, Mercury ingress Pisces 22:49

Today's Venus conjunct Jupiter aspect is a positive sign for your social life. Expect an upward trend as rising prospects draw communication and invitations to mingle. It brings good fortune into your life as you sail on a journey towards nurturing harmony and happiness in your world. An emphasis on sharing with friends and loved ones encourage new goals and projects.

3 Friday

A change of pace brings a refreshing environment. Unexpected developments ahead bring news and invitations to social gatherings. It brings an essential backdrop for getting together with your tribe and sharing discussions that help you create headway towards developing a progressive time of growth. It immerses your energy in a beautiful environment that promotes happiness and harmony.

4 Saturday

A positive trend sets the stage for an enchanting chapter. It does mark a bold beginning for your social life. Moving in alignment with your vision lays the groundwork to improve your circumstances. It shines a spotlight on opportunities to connect with your broader social environment. You cast an enterprising light on your goals. You can use innovative technology to forge a path of connection and abundance.

5 Sunday

Improvement ahead promotes growth around your home and family life. A therapeutic and healing influence motivates positive change in your life. It frees you to engage with life and push back the barriers. A freedom-loving vibe encourages new adventures. It brings various projects and plans which enhance your experience and refine your talents. It does get time to focus on yourself and nurture projects that build bridges of stability in your life.

6 Monday ~ Purim (Begins at sundown), Sun sextile Uranus 13:41

This sextile heightens creativity and self-expression. You discover a new approach that boosts productivity and offers efficiency in your daily life. Change and discovery add a spontaneous element today. Anything could crop up to provide you with a sign of newfound inspiration. You lift the shutters on a chapter that offers room to develop your talents. It does provide side journeys where you can explore a passage towards learning a course along the way.

7 Tuesday ~ Worm Full Moon in Virgo 12:40 Purim (Ends at sunset), Saturn ingress Pisces 13:03

The planet Saturn moving into Pisces is a significant shift. This change of the Saturnian guards highlights the need for spiritual healing. It emphasizes finding meaning in your daily life and growing a solid spiritual basis to help you ride out any turbulence in your life. It brings more balance and harmony to your life, which is therapeutic for your spirit. It rejuvenates your life with lighter energy

8 Wednesday

You chart a course towards a unique territory that draws new friendships to light. You touch down in a social environment that lets you mix and cultivate supportive conversations. Life is a whirlwind of fun possibilities. Light-hearted discussions provide stimulating conversations that inspire your mind. A buzz of activity in your social life brings invitations to mingle. It draws a phase of liberation, freedom, and expansion.

9 Thursday

Life holds a unique twist when news arrives that unearths exciting potential. Seeds planted during this time ripen and blossom over the coming months. It lets you test the water of a new journey, which marks a significant transition towards nurturing an area of interest. It is an excellent time to plan for the future and map your vision. It creates a strategy and a trajectory. It makes for a window of opportunity that improves stability while letting you structure your goals and climb the ladder to success.

10 Friday

Changes ahead bring clear skies overhead. It brings opportunities to socialize, which nurtures your spirit. Breaking free of limitations draws an expansive environment. It's a refreshing change that opens pathways for growth. You can reshuffle the decks of potential by staying open and flexible; it seems something new crosses your path; it connects you with inspiration. It underscores a willingness to develop life by dabbling in a new interest.

11 Saturday ~ Venus sextile Mars 15:04, Mercury sextile Uranus 21:04

Venus has your back today and draws social engagement into your life. A flurry of social opportunities brings mixing with friends, and a happy influence nurtures better foundations in your life. Sharing with cohorts opens the gate to an expressive and expansive time that offers rising prospects. Investing your energy in developing bonds sees a positive return flow into your world. It marks the beginning of an enriching journey that harnesses the essence of harmony.

12 Sunday

Rejuvenation and renewal is a strong theme that surrounds your life. It signifies an ending to stress and worry. It brings people into your life that inspire your spirit. It lets you open the door to a remarkable journey of new possibilities. A refreshing change brings a welcome sense of freedom. It creates a shift forward you can embrace. It does seem you can put your troubles behind you and enjoy a fresh chapter.

13 Monday

You head to a busy chapter with added responsibilities. Your working life moves towards a more demanding environment. It brings a path to securing growth and improving the stability of your foundations. It is a busy time that keeps you on your toes. It lets you settle into a new groove as your efforts garner recognition. It does seem there could be something on offer that takes your abilities to the next level.

14 Tuesday

You are ready to usher in a new journey. It takes your skills to new heights. There is a strong focus ahead on what is truly important to you. It does bring time to work through issues that hold your potential back. Planning the course lets you develop innovative solutions that clear the decks for a fresh start. You approach life with a unique flair that amplifies your success rate.

15 Wednesday ~ Last Q Moon in Sagittarius 2:08, Sun conjunct Neptune 23:39

You may feel sensitivities rising today as the Sun links up with Neptune in the sign of Pisces today. Intuition is sparking; you can trust your gut instincts to guide you correctly when you reveal curious information. Little goes under your radar when you spot an opportunity to improve your circumstances. It brings advancement that lets you appreciate the path forward. New opportunities are around your life, landing you in an environment ripe for an upgrade.

16 Thursday ~ Mercury conjunct Neptune 17:13, Sun square Mars 18:09,
Venus square Pluto 19:58, Venus ingress Taurus 22:31

Today, you may feel chaotic and under pressure as a great deal of cosmic energy disrupts stability in your life. Expect intensity as the Sun square Mars alignment may leave you tense and hot under the collar. Creative expression and taking time to make yourself a priority will be beneficial in releasing frustrations and any heavy energy clinging to your spirit.

17 Friday ~ St Patrick's Day. Mercury square Mars 4:48,
Sun conjunct Mercury 10:45, Venus sextile Saturn 20:25

Today, Venus sextile Saturn promotes cooperation and offers the chance to join a joint project. New options ahead bring choices and decisions. It helps you move past roadblocks and head towards change as you mobilize and extend your reach into a unique area. Life is ready to beam new opportunities into your world. It brings developments that enable you to create progress.

18 Saturday

New possibilities leave you feeling reinvigorated. It opens options that align with future goals. It brings a social aspect that promotes happiness in your life. It raises confidence and draws an expressive time emphasizing sharing authentic and inspiring conversations with people who understand your take on life. Mingling with friends grounds and stabilizes energy, securing a stable platform in your life.

19 Sunday ~ Mercury ingress Aries 4:22

You receive what you need to thrive soon. Blossoming options ahead light an exciting path forward, which draws a journey of connection and companionship. Increasing social engagement promotes insightful discussions that replenish depleted emotional tanks. It opens a self-expressive journey that raises confidence and sees you spending more time with people you value.

20 Monday ~ Sun sextile Pluto 20:12, Sun ingress Aries 21:20,
Ostara/Spring Equinox 21:25

Exploring leads and being proactive rewards a pleasing result that offers heightened security. It cracks the code to a career path that is progressive, dynamic, and ambitious. It brings a role that nurtures abilities and advances talents towards a higher level of achievement. It brings an open road of potential that expands horizons, bringing sweeping changes.

21 Tuesday ~ New Moon in Pisces 17:22

Nurturing your skills advances your abilities into new areas. Your talents are evolving; it brings a chance to share your expertise with a broader audience. It starts a lively and productive chapter that offers a whirlwind of new possibilities. It brings a phase of liberation, freedom, and expansion. It marks a turning point as the changes ahead get the magic flowing into your life. It gives you the green light to pour your energy into growing your career path.

22 Wednesday ~ Ramadan Begins

Significant changes ahead connect you with a prosperous chapter. It offers benefits that shine a light on an expansive and optimistic time of growth in your life. As you develop unique goals that center around your gifts and talents, you promote creativity and amplify the potential possible in your world. It lifts the lid on an inspiring journey that offers a wellspring of goodness.

23 Thursday ~ Pluto ingress Aquarius 8:42

Sifting and sorting options help you spot an opportunity that has been flying under the radar. It helps shift you forward and enjoy a much-appreciated taste of freedom and excitement. Expanding horizons helps open up pathways that feel like a good fit for your restless energy. Jotting down plans and working towards your goals brings rejuvenation and a chance to rebrand your skills in an exciting area worth your time.

24 Friday

News arrives soon that offers a positive aspect. It reveals an exciting possibility that broadens the borders of your world. This information bodes well for developing a new area in your life. It offers a highly productive cycle that promotes expansion as you connect with a broader circle of friends. Forging friendships and getting involved with your social life offers sound foundations with excellent stability and balance.

25 Saturday ~ Mars ingress Cancer 11:36

Becoming true to yourself puts your goals front and center. It brings a prime time for pursuing dreams and soaring towards a greater level of success. Seeing the more substantial possibilities brings the drive and resources to get projects off the ground. Focusing on your most pressing desires brings advancement. It aligns your actions with your highest good, bringing a progressive time of developing your vision for future growth.

26 Sunday

Exploring new interests and developing leads for your life draws an optimistic influence. You touch down on a fascinating landscape that lets you share time with friends and kindred spirits. It brings an uplifting aspect of sharing thoughtful discussions which promote stability and happiness in your life. You can turn a corner and grow your life in an exciting new direction.

27 Monday

An opportunity ahead helps showcase your talents and share your endeavors with a broader audience. Developing creative projects becomes a focal point that places you on the path to advancing your creative skills. A fortunate trend arrives that brings an uptick of potential into your life. It gives you the green light to deepen your knowledge and grow your ideas.

28 Tuesday ~ Mercury conjunct Jupiter 6:49

This astrological conjunct is perfect for brainstorming as ideas are big and expressive under this planetary influence. Having a clear vision of your future goals will do wonders for getting a project off the ground. It lets you step out on a journey of rising possibilities that attracts new beginnings. Increasing your knowledge and developing your talents enables you to grow greener pastures. It promotes expansion and links you up with an engaging social environment.

29 Wednesday ~ First Quarter Moon in Cancer 2:32

An opportunity ahead brings the gift of rising prospects. Your willingness to explore leads draws a bonus. It sparks clear skies overhead and encourages you to lift the barriers that limit progress in your life. You tap into developing areas that soothe your soul and heighten your well-being in your world. It paves the way toward an exciting chapter of prosperity and renewal.

30 Thursday ~ Mars trine Saturn 19:03, Venus conjunct Uranus 22:25

Mars forms a trine with Saturn today to give your working life wings. Hard work, dedication, and perseverance improve the day-to-day foundations of your life. Venus teams up with Uranus to add a dash of spontaneity to your social/personal life. As you embark on a new adventure, staying true to yourself will keep you aligned with the person you are becoming.

APRIL

Sun	Mon	Tue	Wed	Thu	Fri	Sat
						1
2	3	4	5	6	7	8
9	10	11	12	13	14	15
16	17	18	19	20	21	22
23	24	25	26	27	28	29
30						

New Moon

PINK MOON

31 Friday

A focus on rebuilding foundations brings stability and balance. It leads to a busy time that sees headway occurring around larger goals. It triggers a stable phase of growth that sets the right tone to help things come together with intention. It does smooth out the road's bumps and lets the journey progress towards a more abundant landscape. It speaks of increased potential around home life. It brings grounded energy that restores balance.

1 Saturday ~ All Fools/April Fool's Day

Notable changes ahead promote a journey that nurtures your life. It helps you cross the threshold and transition towards a time of self-development and growth. A significant turning point occurs as a social aspect connects with kinship and companionship. It draws a positive influence that secures stable foundations. Sharing with treasured companions highlights a supportive environment that promotes happiness.

2 Sunday ~ Palm Sunday.

The power of magic currently surrounds your broader circle of friends. Life becomes a blaze of activity when invitations arrive that draw lively energy into your world. It creates space to deepen bonds, seeing life bloom with fresh possibilities. It brings unscripted adventures into your life that promote stimulating conversations. It offers fun and happiness as goodness surrounds your life.

3 Monday ~ Mercury ingress Taurus 16:20

Your ideas and vision for the future have gained traction. It draws stability and heightens security in your world. It is a journey that offers abundance, transformation, and growth. Something is on offer that elevates your role to a new level. It brings a chapter that gives you something to celebrate. Productive dialogues draw open communication; this is vital and productive. It helps you focus your energy on an area that offers substantial growth.

4 Tuesday

Your creativity is increasing; this stirs the pot of potential and tempts you towards developing your skills further. It leads to a rich and expressive environment that allows you to harness your energy into areas that offer growth and abundance. If you have been struggling with uncertainty, this resolves as the path ahead clears and beckons you into new territory.

5 Wednesday ~ Passover (begins at sunset), Mercury sextile Saturn 16:18

With Mercury in sextile with Saturn, communication skills are rising. Enhanced clarity and mental insight help you understand more significant concepts, thought processes, and ideas with ease today. This cosmic enhancement enables you to step beyond traditional or repetitive learning. Confidence is increasing, allowing you to upgrade your working life and meet any demands on the to-do list.

6 Thursday ~ Lent Ends. Pink Full Moon in Libra 4:37

Trimming the deadwood tree helps you manifest a new start. Complexities surrounding your life dissipate, and you enjoy more grounded foundations. It has you moving towards an expressive, dynamic, and happy landscape. It brings a shakeup that releases outworn energy and rejuvenates your life from the ground up. A time of restructuring draws changes that guide the path forward.

7 Friday ~ Good Friday, Venus sextile Neptune 17: 59

Today's planetary alignment offers a mindful, spiritual aspect that is in keeping with the spirit of Easter. Venus sends loving beams into your home and family life, harmonizing bonds and drawing the essence of rejuvenation and renewal. You benefit from a sense of rejuvenation from a quiet downturn. If you have been feeling adrift, focusing on foundations restores equilibrium. It shifts you towards an abundant mindset and offers to improve your circumstances.

8 Saturday ~ Mercury sextile Mars 6:23

A sextile between Mercury and Mars sharpens cognitive abilities today. Mental clarity is on the rise, giving you valuable insight into the path ahead. You come from a long line of trailblazers and should invest in your talents. Using your abilities brings goodness to the top. Something new and tempting arrives, and it brings a breakthrough. A breath of fresh air renews your energy, drawing rejuvenation. It takes you toward an expansive and happy chapter.

9 Sunday ~Easter Sunday

It is a powerful time for growing your world as new information flows into your life which lights up pathways of rising prospects. News arrives that earmarks a unique beginning in your life. It ushers in a busy time that opens a social phase. It brings networking and invitations, which help you plug into a social environment that offers support and connection. Exploring a community setting with friends nurtures well-being and happiness in your life.

10 Monday

Life picks up steam, and events ahead set in motion exciting opportunities for your life. Curious changes along bring improvement of circumstances which feels heartening. It lights a social environment that grows your world and tempts you to cross the threshold and enter a brighter chapter in your life. A change of scenery rejuvenates and renews your energy. It promotes lively discussions, which trigger a highly creative atmosphere.

11 Tuesday ~ Venus ingress Gemini 4:43, Venus trine Pluto 10:14, Sun Conjunct Jupiter 22:07, Mercury at Greatest Elong 19.5E

The Sun lights the path ahead. It helps you advance a long-term goal when an influx of potential sees a surge of motivation flow into your world. Gaining insight into your future vision illuminates a course that takes you towards growth. You see improvements in the areas of home life and social circle. It kickstarts a bountiful chapter that sees you involved with a cooperative venture.

12 Wednesday

Life brings a significant shift forward as the path ahead clears, and opportunities weave into a golden aspect of your life. It offers an enriching time that brings a quickening of pace to your social life. Sharing thoughts with like-minded people nurture stability and happiness in your life. Unexpected serendipity brings companionship and kinship as a meeting of the minds draws close talks.

13 Thursday ~ Passover (ends at sunset), Last Quarter Moon in Capricorn 9:11

News arrives that bodes well for your dreams. It is a fruitful time for expansion. It brings a highly productive cycle that offers opportunities to socialize. As you surround yourself with the right type of people and positive energy, you enter a time of renewal and rejuvenation. Abundant life options draw stability and improve the building blocks of your foundations. It is a time for setting intentions and thinking about your long-term vision.

14 Friday ~ Orthodox Good Friday, Venus square Saturn 16:38

A Venus square Saturn encourages taking a personal inventory of meaningful areas in your life. Adjusting courses as necessary will give private bonds the best chance of success. Shining a more intensive light on interpersonal situations in your social life helps cut away from outworn areas. Set firm boundaries if a drama llama is in your circle of friends. Not everyone is deserving of your time and attention. Saturn will help you trim the deadwood holding you back.

15 Saturday

It is a busy time that brings an end to disappointment. It offers new adventures that inspire and delight. It brings a highly social environment that connects you with a crew of innovative characters. You invest your energy in a situation that offers room to progress. It does bring a time of heightened creativity and enterprising options. You enter a growth cycle that takes your vision to a new level.

16 Sunday ~ Orthodox Easter

You enter the high-energy and social chapter that brings engagement and support. It brings the kind of changes you are seeking. It does see sunny skies overhead, and abundance flows into your life. It brings a refreshing social aspect that offers a wellspring of harmony and joy—sharing experiences with another lightens the path to a more connected future. You see, the advancement nourishes your spirit; it brings positive energy into your life.

17 Monday

The future is looking brighter all the time. Life turns the corner and heads to an upswing. It brings an optimistic phase of developing goals. You reach a turning point, and this pushes back barriers. It unleashes your abilities in an area ripe for advancement. Removing the drama by placing appropriate barriers clears the path ahead. It brings solutions; it unleashes creativity and makes the magic flow freely in your world.

18 Tuesday

Life offers the chance to follow your vision soon. You have more control over the road ahead than you may currently understand. A new start flows into your life; plenty of activity afoot shines a light on a productive growth phase. It creates a strong basis from which to journey forward. It makes you feel inspired and ready to take on new responsibilities enthusiastically. Refining your talents sharpens your skills; it shines a light on new possibilities.

19 Wednesday

Focusing on the basics takes you to the building blocks of life. As you peel back the layers, you reveal the refreshing potential that expands your situation. It revolutionizes your environment and draws enthusiasm. It puts you in charge of proactively nurturing your environment and harnessing the power of manifestation to advance life. It marks a new beginning when an ample opportunity tempts you forward. Communication arrives to get the ball rolling.

20 Thursday ~ Ramadan Ends, New Moon in Taurus 4:12, Hybrid Solar Eclipse, Sun ingress Taurus 8:09, Sun square Pluto 16:26

The Sun square Pluto aspect draws renewal and rejuvenation. Pluto charts a course towards transformation and offers a highly creative part that lights the way forward towards improving your circumstances. The Sun contributes to golden beams that offer harmony, transcendence, and rising prospects. This planetary combo elevates creative inclinations due to a New Moon today.

21 Friday ~ Mercury turns Retrograde in Taurus at 8:34

Mercury plays havoc with interpersonal bonds and can send communication haywire during its retrograde phase. Buckle up; it will be a bumpy ride as your social life goes on a Mercury-driven rollercoaster. If someone's contact triggers an emotional aspect, be mindful that this planetary phase is best with a balanced and understanding approach. As you navigate forward, being adaptable, compassionate, and flexible will help stabilize personal bonds.

22 Saturday ~ Earth Day, Lyrids Meteor Shower from April 16th -25th

You move forward towards a fresh start. It is a catalyst for growth as it opens new options to tempt you. It rules the way of expansion that brings new people into your life. Expanding your network of support multiplies the goodness in your world. It advances you forward to a more connected and lively environment. It brings confidence, which makes you more assertive about what you need in your life.

23 Sunday

Indeed, examining the path ahead brings a life journey worth exploring. You reveal secret information that opens the way forward. A piece of the puzzle falls into place, opening new areas. It does unleash your abilities in an area that inspires your mind. It brings an assignment for your talents; it represents a fluid and changing environment that offers side paths. Exploring these diverging routes brings an exciting shift forward.

24 Monday ~ Mercury sextile Mars 3:22

Quick reflexes enable you to spot the diamond in the rough. The Mercury sextile with Mars offers new leads. You benefit from changes ahead as an original and exciting journey opens life up. You discover the correct elements to thrive in a unique landscape that promotes skill development. Refining your abilities draws advancement. It lets you take on an enterprising area that offers rising prospects. You soon build stable foundations which heighten the security around your life.

25 Tuesday ~ Sun sextile Saturn 10:47

Today's sextile brings opportunities that light a path forward. It illuminates fantastic potential that enables you to improve your circumstances. A side avenue opens and brings a unique trail that promotes your abilities and deepens your talents. Dabbling in areas that inspire you creatively keeps life lively and fresh. It's an enterprising time that offers a wellspring of possibility in your life—moving beyond your everyday routine ushers in new adventures.

26 Wednesday

As you progress, you enter a productive and robust chapter that elevates prospects in your world. It hits a high note as you unearth new possibilities. It brings a landmark phase of progressing your dreams. Your abilities grow by leaps and bounds as you navigate a path towards your vision. Streamlining, planning, and prioritizing draw dividends. The decisions you make bring an approach worth growing. You enter an ambitious cycle that holds great promise.

27 Thursday ~ First Quarter Moon in Leo 21:20

Driving your energy in a focused manner lets you achieve growth. It marks a significant time when change is possible. You are supported to reach for your dreams and develop your goals. Exciting visions of a future destination guide this process, letting you dream big and go for a pinnacle. You meet someone edgy and outspoken; this person becomes a guide and mentor who assists this growth and learning journey.

28 Friday

Today anchors you to a productive chapter that is active and lively. It draws transformation and happiness. It does see new information arrives; it lets you carve out space to nurture your talents. A whirlwind of potential brings your life a boost. An experimental flavor heightens creativity as you create the winning factor. Your situation is changing and evolving; this brings new people into your life. It offers a social aspect that is reinvigorating.

29 Saturday ~ Mars sextile Uranus 8:04

This sextile brings unique ideas that help you think outside the box to obtain innovative solutions. Uranus places the focus on rebellion, liberation, and freedom. It adds a dash of spontaneity to your life today. A peak of creative energy is ahead, and this draws new possibilities. It brings an active and vibrant chapter. It takes you towards a highly self-expressive and creative environment. It does position you correctly to achieve growth and progress your vision.

30 Sunday

Events unfold over the coming days that draw harmony. It connects you with a compelling journey of developing emotional bonds. It brings an enriching chapter that offers a fresh start to your life. It is a process of tearing down outworn energy and revealing the new growth ready to blossom in your life. Making informed choices lets you ascertain the right path to journey down. It does get the ball rolling on a social chapter that brings improvement to your life.

MAY

Sun	Mon	Tue	Wed	Thu	Fri	Sat
	1	2	3	4	5	6
7	8	9	10	11	12	13
14	15	16	17	18	19	20
21	22	23	24	25	26	27
28	29	30	31			

AQUARIUS
VIRGO
TAURUS
STARS
SCORPIO
MARS
SUN
ARIES
WEDDING
WEALTH
FORTUNE
CAPRICORN
CALENDAR
GEMINI
LOVE
ASTROLOGY
HOROSCOPE
MONTH
MOON
LEO
SAGITTARIUS
HAPPINESS
ASTRONOMY
CANCER
LIBRA
BIRTHDAY
DATE
ZODIAC
NEPTUNE
PISCES
SKY
EARTH
SIGN
TODAY
DAILY
WEEKLY
CONSTELLATION
MONTHLY

NEW MOON

FLOWER MOON

1 Monday ~ Beltane/May Day, Pluto turns retrograde in Aquarius 18:39, Sun conjunct Mercury 23:27

Pluto is the modern ruler of Scorpio; it symbolizes how we experience power, renewal, rebirth, and mysterious or subconscious forces. This retrograde phase lasts until October. It allows you to dive deep and explore inner realms and darker aspects of your personality ordinarily hidden from view. Understanding your psyche deeper provides access to the forces driving your personality. It lets you comprehend the why and wherefore behind desires.

2 Tuesday

You can create peace by focusing on the more minor things in your life. It gives you back control and stability. You soon find your groove by going with the flow. It brings balance and immersing yourself in grounded energy lets you focus on areas that hold meaning. It brings a time of heightened creativity that hits the right note for your life. A metamorphosis brings transformation and a new path forward. It brings a turning point that offers growth.

3 Wednesday

You are ready for new adventures, and expanding your life becomes a top priority. It does connect you to endeavors and projects you can develop and grow. There's an opportunity to collaborate and achieve a team approach. It brings an influx of work, which indicates that the tides are turning in your favor. As you launch into this busy and productive time, it helps you put plans together that offer a chance to learn and grow your abilities.

4 Thursday ~ Venus square Neptune 17:40

A Venus square Neptune aspect offers a dreamy quality. It provides the perfect vibe for engaging in the big sky and dreaming about your perfect romantic escapade. While fairytales in the sky offer relaxation and escapism, it's important to remember that this dreaminess could lead to delusion if you overly focus on something out of reach. Understanding the escapism and creative elements at play enables you to dream big and still feel grounded in reality.

5 Friday ~ Venus sextile Jupiter 4:02, Flower Full Moon in Scorpio 17:34 Penumbral Lunar Eclipse

A Venus and Jupiter sextile creates beneficial and harmonious vibrations for your romantic life. Good luck, and rising prospects bring warmth and social engagement. It takes you to a radiant chapter that offers gifts of self-expression. It provides a social and freedom-loving chapter of connecting with friends. Life sparkles with options that help you improve your love life.

6 Saturday ~ Eta Aquarids Meteor Shower April 19th - May 28th

You have energy that strengthens your spirit and elevates your potential more than you currently realize. As you expand your life, you double up on creativity and stir up new goals to light the way forward. Life is changing; you benefit from being flexible and adaptable. It is a significant time for self-discovery and growth. You connect with others who join you to usher in new energy and fresh possibilities. You land in an environment ripe for growing your dreams.

7 Sunday ~ Venus ingress Cancer 14:20

Being mindful of your goals creates a path that draws abundance. Attractive opportunities make a powerful lure that inspires your mind. The energy of magic surrounds your environment as you benefit from events on the horizon. It brings communication that highlights a social and welcoming aspect. It lets you recharge and thrive in an abundant landscape. It brings social engagement that connects you with the lighter side of life.

8 Monday

You head to a time of heightened creativity and self-expression. There is a spotlight on progressing long-term goals. Focusing on your priorities offers the chance to grow your situation robustly. Your ability to manifest and improve your life is evolving, which brings advancement. Little goes under your radar as you embrace an influx of potential. It lets you set sail on a voyage that draws happiness and abundance.

9 Tuesday ~ Sun conjunct Uranus 19:55

You see the world through a beginner's eyes as you recapture a sense of innocence and excitement. Pursuing dreams, and being open to meeting new people, bring expansive horizons into your life. It is a time of remarkable personal growth, self-development, and fresh adventures to grow your world and deepen your knowledge. It brings new people into your life who offer vibrant conversations and a unique take on life.

10 Wednesday

You discover a slow and steady approach offers progress in your life. You build your goals carefully, and attention to detail brings sustainable results which carry you forward and improve your circumstances. Pausing to reflect and gather your resources before embarking on your next journey lets you plan the path correctly. You see a broader overview as you contemplate and consider future goals before deciding on a course of action.

11 Thursday

A new phase of life triggers rejuvenation and renewal. It highlights a community environment that lets you connect with like-minded people. Pouring your energy into your social life draws support and thoughtful discussions. It brings a happy time that enables you to advance life towards greener pastures. Life-affirming invitations connect you with kindred spirits.

12 Friday ~ Mercury sextile Saturn 8:32, Last Quarter Moon in Aquarius 14:28

Mercury sextile Saturn boosts your Friday, which helps you tidy up loose ends before the weekend. Mental acuity rises, bringing a focused mind, and increased powers of observation lets you see what needs addressing. Today's other cognitive improvements include excellent concentration, memory, and organization skills. With everything running smoothly in your working life, you can enjoy the weekend ahead, knowing you have taken care of your business.

13 Saturday ~ Mercury sextile Venus 2:41, Venus trine Saturn 6:56

Mercury sextile Venus offers a social and friendly influence making this a great day to connect with your tribe. You can accomplish great things by being open to new experiences and situations. Life supports your journey towards expanding your social life. It brings a busy time where you have options to draw a unique companion into your inner circle. It allows you to share thoughts and ideas with a kindred spirit.

14 Sunday ~ Mother's Day (US)

Things are on the move soon. It brings many opportunities into your life and may spark a new direction. Underneath this energy is a desire to advance your circumstances forward. You benefit from the positive energy that arrives to stir up creativity and get the ball rolling on a new interest area. It brings a sweet influence that brings time for friends and family.

15 Monday ~ Mercury turns direct in Taurus 3:16, Mars trine Neptune 13:44

With Mercury turning direct today, the focus is on your social life. Mars forms a trine with Neptune, enhancing potential as confidence rises and you feel ready for social engagement. It offers the perfect solution for the dodgems as you get busy being self-expressive, communicative, and creative. A curious mind and an open heart enable you to throw caution to the wind and embrace new challenges and experiences in your life.

16 Tuesday ~ Jupiter ingress Taurus 17:01

The seeds you plant over the coming months become the cycle that launches your talents to the next level. You discover a higher realm of possibilities and soon rise to the occasion. Using your abilities and being resourceful opens pathways of expression and creativity. It rewards with tangible results and options which inspire growth. Tapping into the potential around your life brings a fresh zest that boosts morale.

17 Wednesday

You put your worries and troubles behind you and take advantage of the wisdom you learned to forge a path aligned with your vision. It begins a voyage that captures the essence of wanderlust. Adventure and excitement pave the way forward. It has you feeling energized about the potential possible in your life. You make a wise choice, and this opens the path to plenty. It is a time that opens a gateway toward exciting possibilities.

18 Thursday ~ Jupiter square Pluto 1:09, Sun sextile Neptune 8:59

Today's Jupiter square Pluto brings extra drive and increased energy to complete projects and finish your to-do list. Neptune also boosts your goals as a sextile with the Sun helps you find the resources and support needed to manifest your vision. You can bring your dreams to reality as the planets have your back today, attracting rising prospects into your life. You move towards developing an endeavor that enhances your abilities.

19 Friday ~ Mercury sextile Saturn 6:50 New Moon in Taurus 15:54

Today, Mercury, Saturn sextile boosts your communication skills and confidence. Add in a dash of New Moon inspiration and aspiration, and you have the perfect mix for engaging in brainstorming with valued companions. Sharing ideas and adding creative ingredients into the pot of manifestation helps you develop a winning trajectory from which to grow your world next month.

20 Saturday ~ Mars ingress Leo 15:24

Mars lands in Leo, and this raises confidence. It's time to go big and be proud and bold. You head towards an uptick in the potential for your social life. It brings companionship and kinship into your life. Being intentional and developing your dreams allow you to open new doors for your personal life. Intelligent choices and decisions bring success and stability into your life. Growing your life banishes the clouds and brings new possibilities.

21 Sunday ~ Mars opposed Pluto 3:11, Sun ingress Gemini 7:04, Sun trine Pluto 13:58

Mars connects with a competitive edge today that could see your authority tested. The Sun trine Pluto aspect also fuels the fire, increasing your desire to gain power and feed your ambitious streak. You seek opportunities to elevate your standing among peers and co-workers today. Climbing the ladder towards success becomes a dominant factor.

22 Monday ~ Victoria Day (Canada), Sun sextile Mars 5:56

The Sun sextile Mars transit brings vital energy and renewed zest for life. You enter a time of transformation that lifts your spirits higher. The troubles of the past no longer block the journey ahead. It brings a clean sweep of potential that offers growth, advancement, and results. The sun shines brightly over your world as you embark on a journey that sets your heart ablaze with excitement. New opportunities are afoot; life holds change and discovery overhead.

23 Tuesday ~ Mars square Jupiter 5:13

Today's Mars square Jupiter offers a positive influence that increases stamina and boosts your energy. Enthusiasm for the task at hand rises, boosting productivity and enabling you to deal with the day's demands efficiently and capably. Investigating an area of interest opens a path you can explore to your advantage. A new option emerges and paints a picture of abundance. It does bring a time of news and communication.

24 Wednesday

Something comes to fruition that inspires your mind. It does advance you forward and could bring a big announcement or celebration that brings joy. It is a fast-moving environment that lets you tap into pathways of growth. It communicates that you can expand your horizons and explore new possibilities. Something in the pipeline creates a stir of excitement. It shows a favorable aspect that beautifully orients you to a path of plenty.

25 Thursday ~ Shavuot (Begins at sunset)

Your life has undergone some rapid changes, and taking time to process your changing emotional landscape helps nurture well-being and harmony. Research ahead brings a passageway towards growth. It brings a time of new beginnings into your life. It renews your spirit and opens your eyes to a broader world of potential around your life. It begins a new journey that offers room to advance your world and grow your life in a refreshing direction.

26 Friday ~ Venus sextile Uranus 7:36

Today's sextile promotes a vibrant and active social life. With Venus charming and Uranus adding a dash of spontaneity to your weekend plans, it assures a fun and lively time shared with friends. News arrives that charms and inspires. It brings changes that restore balance as it shifts your focus forward. It does grow your social life and brings opportunities to mingle. It opens a path to developing a situation of interest. It takes you on a journey of happiness and harmony.

27 Saturday ~ Shavuot (Ends at sunset), First Quarter Moon in Virgo 15:22

You can expect an influx of potential to emerge in your social life soon. Suppose you feel life's challenges. In that case, this enables you to build your emotional foundation through a sense of connection and support with others who understand you on a deeper level. As you close the door to a problematic chapter, the stress melts away. It brings opportunities and options into your life. Planning your goals creates a turning point that takes you toward your vision.

28 Sunday

You benefit from more excellent stability that draws a firm basis to your foundations. It focuses on practical matters around home and family life. It kickstarts a chapter that emphasizes practical issues. As you improve your bottom line, you branch out and develop other areas of your life. It does create a ripple effect of abundance around your situation. It brings a chance to socialize that offers improvement.

JUNE

Sun	Mon	Tue	Wed	Thu	Fri	Sat
				1	2	3
4	5	6	7	8	9	10
11	12	13	14	15	16	17
18	19	20	21	22	23	24
25	26	27	28	29	30	

NEW MOON

STRAWBERRY MOON

29 Monday ~ Memorial Day, Mercury at Greatest Elongation 24.9W

It is a time of change on many levels. Something new and exciting emerges that brings good fortune into your world. Store outdated areas on the back burner and let other projects come sharply into focus. You've had enough of backtracking; a change in direction ahead provides an impressive route forward. An endeavor set in motion offers a good result that boosts your confidence. An emphasis on improving your circumstances lights a progressive path ahead.

30 Tuesday

You are on a journey of growth and evolution. It helps expand the barriers and lets you explore new horizons. It brings a path of inspiration and potential. Helpful news arrives that points the way forward. It brings great excitement and helps you remove limiting beliefs around security. It lets you blaze through towards achieving a stage of growth that heightens the potential possible. Releasing blocks nurtures creativity.

31 Wednesday

The way to achieve growth in your life is to lean into challenges. When things feel tough, it indicates you are growing your abilities. The more you expand your life, the more challenging aspects become before you achieve a higher level of success. It does take your talents to the next level, and life will smooth out along the way.

1 Thursday

A goal you have been hoping to achieve reaches fruition soon. It brings a confidence-boosting journey that pushes back the barriers as you develop your life in a unique direction. Gathering your resources, you open your world to a myriad of possibilities that help you create a shift of forwarding motion. It brings an essential time to get involved in growing your world.

2 Friday ~ Venus trine Neptune 22:42

Creativity and imagination are peaking under the blissful Venus, Neptune trine. Harmony, equilibrium, and well-being soar under this positive influence. Self-expression is rising, cultivating a unique path that captures the essence of artistic inclinations. Venus showers positivity over your social life, improving personal bonds. Curiosity leads to an uplifting time discussing future projects and endeavors with a kindred spirit who understands your outlook on life.

3 Saturday

Changes ahead keep you on your toes. It brings a busy and active chapter, which offers room to improve your social life. You draw unique people into your world. Your ability to nurture friendships and bonds is rising; this attracts the right kind of people. It lets you create a bridge towards a happy and supported future. A refreshing change is coming that opens high potential around your social life.

4 Sunday ~ Strawberry Full Moon in Sagittarius 3:42,
Mercury conjunct Uranus 19:50

Mercury and Uranus form a positive aspect that heightens mental abilities. Increasing mental stimulation promotes fresh ideas in your life today. Technology, messages, and communication all spark inspiration and foster possibilities for future development. It brings innovative conversations where you begin working towards a project involving collaboration.

5 Monday ~ Venus ingress Leo 13:42, Venus opposed Pluto 16:04

Pursuing opportunities brings an enterprising time of exploring exciting prospects. Your willingness to be open to new leads becomes part of a more extensive chapter of growth that takes you towards unique interests. It brings a purposeful journey of refining your skills and connecting with others who understand and support your goals. It opens a gateway forward, which helps you map out new plans for development.

6 Tuesday

There is plenty of excitement ahead. It does see you diverging from your everyday routine. New responsibilities and options inspire growth. It does see you working with your skills and refining your abilities. Don't be afraid to extend your reach into new areas. It is a valuable tool that grows your abilities. Putting the shine on your talents gets your work noticed. It brings recognition and offers a chance to develop your abilities in a new area fully.

7 Wednesday

There is plenty of potential coming into your world. It helps you move forward with new goals and an inspiring vision of future possibilities. Implementing functional changes enables you to take the steps necessary to grow your life in a structured and balanced manner. It offers foundations that are stable and prosperous. You can shuffle the decks of potential and come up with a winner. Abundance is a theme that resonates with optimism throughout your world.

8 Thursday

It's a great time to map out goals. A willingness to explore new possibilities opens a unique road. Intuition and creativity flow into your world to assist a journey forward. There are developments around your life that bring the building blocks of stability. The time is ripe to progress your vision and align your thoughts toward future possibilities. Prioritizing goals streamlines the path; it captures the essence of efficiency.

9 Friday

A surprise arrives with a burst of excitement and news. It opens new pathways to bond with kindred spirits. It's a chapter of fresh beginnings that leaves you feeling inspired. It brings a positive note that offers a social aspect. A wellspring of abundance blossoms as you dive into refreshing conversations that speak to your heart. It's a chance to grow your social circle, which starts a dynamic phase.

10 Saturday ~ Last Quarter Moon in Pisces 19:31

You are ready to open a new chapter in your social life. Mingling and networking with friends offer an active and productive environment. It attracts a suitable landscape for you to thrive. Something in the pipeline emerges and hits a sweet note for your dreams. It is the giver of renewal and happiness as it lights up pathways that improve friendships and social bonds. Invitations and news stir up excitement.

11 Sunday ~ Mercury ingress Gemini 10:24, Mercury trine Pluto 10:27, Pluto ingress Capricorn 13:12, Venus square Jupiter 15:39

Today's Venus square Jupiter planetary alignment offers good things for your social life. It is the perfect time to engage with friends; lively discussions nurture creativity. It is a prime time for letting your hair down and having fun in a relaxing environment that draws stability into your world.

12 Monday

Old challenges melt away under sunny skies. It brings a bright time filled with energy and enthusiasm. It has you reaching for your goals; the timing is right for expansion. It launches a new enterprise, and this venture improves your chances of success. Your determination to nail your vision brings blossoming activity. A project you invest your energy into jumps to life with new possibilities. It brings advancement that carries you forward.

13 Tuesday

It brings a time of expansion that offers room to progress in your life. Sudden news arrives one day; it sees new potential flowing into your life. It brings a goal-orientated chapter where you find solutions, and hurdles fall by the wayside. Keeping focused on implementing strategic plans provide you with stable foundations. New prospects overhead keep you feeling inspired. It lets you brew up a storm of manifestation with kindred spirits.

14 Wednesday ~ Flag Day

Life becomes a whirlwind, most positively. It lets you cut away from areas that are no longer relevant. It removes the drama and stress. Spending time in the community brings fresh energy to your social life. It draws new opportunities and adventures that inspire personal growth. You thrive in a more social environment, which brings you a treasured companion.

15 Thursday

Some exciting changes ahead will see you moving in a new direction. Your ability to keep things running while implementing new strategies draws dividends. You are ready to transition to a happier chapter; good things are coming. It brings structure and stability, taking your skills to a new level. It sees you working more brilliantly and joining forces with others.

16 Friday

An uptick of opportunities illuminates fantastic potential as you explore pathways that interest you. Tweaking your talents places you in prime alignment to advance your abilities to the next level. As you expand life outwardly, you weave a web of connectedness in your social life, which brings grounded foundations. You light up a journey of social engagement and expansion that widens your world's borders.

17 Saturday ~ Saturn turns Retrograde in Pisces 16:52

Saturn is a planet that rules boundaries, structure, and discipline. This retrograde draws balance and righteousness into your situation. Making reasonable choices and decisions connects with karma to achieve a fair and beneficial outcome. Facing the truth of a situation shines a light on where the scales may be tipped unevenly to one side, creating a sense of imbalance in your life.

18 Sunday ~ New Moon in Cancer 4:38, Father's Day (US)

The New Moon's potential flow leads to a revolution and rejuvenation phase. It lights a positive trend that gives you the confidence to expand your horizons and get the ball rolling on improving your circumstances. Complications fade away, bringing with them the sunshine into your world. You open a bevy of potential and can embrace a more active and social environment. It brings new options that trigger a cascade of possibilities in your mind's eye.

19 Monday ~ Sun square Neptune 3:53, Jupiter sextile Saturn 15:53

Today, the Neptune square Sun aspect can water down your ambitions, leaving you feeling foggy and indecisive. If your vision feels clouded, going back over your plans can help make sure they continue to align with your vision for future growth. Recommitting to develop your career goals can help shift some of the clouds that hang over your working life today. If the boss gives you a hard time, blame it on Neptune for bringing Monday woes into your working life.

20 Tuesday

It is a time of releasing negativity and wiping the slate clean for a new chapter of potential. It offers a great chance to improve and advance your situation forward. Lovely perks crop up that provide a beneficial path toward growth. This opportunity's magical aspect helps you progress a long-held dream that you never previously realized. Your efforts reach fruition, which places you in a position to continue expanding the boundaries and drawing in new goals.

21 Wednesday ~ Midsummer/Litha Solstice 14:58, Mercury sextile Mars 15:23

The Mercury sextile Mars aspect today fosters joint projects and cooperation. Getting involved with a group endeavor stimulates your mind and brings new possibilities. Brainstorming sessions offer a trailblazing path towards innovative solutions and rising prospects. Joining forces and strategizing with like-minded people cultivate an excellent success rate. It helps you cover the bases by blending other people's talents into the mix of potential at your disposal.

22 Thursday

As you move away from the past, you attract options that take your vision forward. It places you in an environment that propels your attention to new possibilities. An active time of socializing ahead brings the perfect chapter the stepping out into a community environment. It lets you make tracks towards nurturing new friendships. It draws a companion who plays an essential role in future events.

23 Friday

Today provides new options that open a gateway toward growth. Being receptive to change lets you flex your talents and take in new areas which offer rising prospects. A pioneering attitude blazes a path towards new adventures. It sets off a brilliant chain of events that draws prosperity and abundance into your world. It lets you focus on building your foundations from the ground up. You turn the corner and illuminate a glorious fresh start.

24 Saturday

Expanding your horizons and opening life up to a more diverse array of possibilities draws a pleasing result for your life. You connect with unique people who support your life, and this expansion gathers a sense of connection for your circle of friends. Experimenting with new pathways draws confidence, leaving you feeling stronger and happier about growing your life. It motivates change and ramps up potential in your personal life.

25 Sunday

You may be feeling as though life has put the brakes on your plans. Facing a crossroads, you face challenges and choose a path that gives you the luck and grace to move forward. It lights a brilliant way that shines abundance upon your home and family life. Progress starts with a grassroots movement that occurs on the home front. It stabilizes foundations and shores up rocky areas, bringing the stability needed to move forward.

26 Monday ~ First Quarter Moon in Libra 7:50, Mars square Uranus 9:22

You benefit from developments on the horizon. It brings blessings as you head towards a productive chapter that is lively and dynamic. It's a busy time that helps you build solid foundations that nurture a stable phase of growth and prosperity. It leaves you feeling optimistic about the future. New inspiration sweeps into your life that clears the path forward. A window of opportunity opens, bringing new possibilities to light.

27 Tuesday ~ Mercury ingress Cancer 12:22

It is a beautiful time to nurture your abilities and plot the course toward your vision. A new project emerges that brings an exciting phase of expansion. It is a time of sudden developments and surprises that culminates in a celebration. Heightened energy brings a burst of new motivation that offers substantial progress. It does get you a change of direction, but this lets you focus on a significant area.

28 Wednesday

Doing your research draws rewarding dividends. It brings a refreshing direction that lets you put your plan for future growth in place. Initiating your vision places you in a solid position to move forward and progress your dreams. It strongly correlates to improved security and improvement on the home front. It lets you focus on creating the change that improves your bottom line. It lets you focus on long-term prospects as your decisions shape your destiny.

29 Thursday ~ Sun trine Saturn 1:42

Today's Sun trine Saturn offers constructive dialogues and thoughtful ideas that enhance your creativity and stimulate new pathways of possibility in your life. A positive influence nurtures unique approaches that capitalize on the potential possible in your surroundings. This beautiful symmetry in the coming chapter heals the past and brings an environment that promotes your abilities. It creates space to dabble in a new interest.

July

Sun	Mon	Tue	Wed	Thu	Fri	Sat
						1
2	3	4	5	6	7	8
9	10	11	12	13	14	15
16	17	18	19	20	21	22
23	24	25	26	27	28	29
30	31					

New Moon

BUCK MOON

30 Friday ~ Neptune turns Retrograde in Pisces, 19:28

Neptune retrograde strips away delusions, allusions, and fanciful thinking. Under the glare of more informed thought processes, you build tangible growth pathways to take your talents to the next level. This phase lets you sink your teeth into developing goals that offer fruitful results. Moving away from areas that have clouded your thinking and brought doubt to your judgment does provide you with clear stepping stones that take you towards success.

1 Saturday ~ Canada Day, Sun conjunct Mercury 5:05, Mercury sextile Jupiter 7:10, Sun sextile Jupiter 10:26

Open-mindedness, curiosity, and a quest for adventure are prominent aspects as a Mercury sextile Jupiter alignment fosters creativity and self-expression. This transit favors organization, planning, and the development of longer-term goals. Reviewing plans and streamlining your vision enables you to cut to the chase and find a practical path to progress your goals. New information emerges to catch your interest and spur you to advance your life.

2 Sunday ~ Venus square Uranus 14:32

An increased need for freedom and liberation can destabilize as Venus faces Uranus in a square alignment. Being mindful of balancing interpersonal bonds while being self-expressive and creative can ease tensions. At the same time, you can let your hair down and enjoy a freedom-driven chapter of fun and excitement. Pushing past perceived limitations reveals a unique possibility for your life.

3 Monday ~ Super Moon, Buck Full Moon in Capricorn 11:40

This Full Moon can feel jarring, and creating space to release outworn areas helps nurture a time of renewal and rejuvenation. It brings the chance to cut away from areas that are no longer part of the journey. Clearing the blocks around your life helps you establish new foundations. It lets you grow a journey that nurtures a wellspring of abundance as you shape new goals. Fanning the flames of inspiration brings creative opportunities that boost your talents.

4 Tuesday ~ Independence Day

The changes ahead bring expansion. It sets a refreshing trend that offers room to grow the path onwards into a meaningful journey. The seeds you plant marks a new beginning. It brings opportunities to develop a more prosperous home and family life. A creative undertaking takes shape and begins to branch out into different areas. It gets you a broader audience that offers feedback and recognition.

5 Wednesday

New possibilities ahead bring change and excitement flowing into your world, helping you build greater security in your life. An active phase of developing new interests taps into a busy time that nurtures your talents. It lights a progressive path that offers a wellspring of prosperity. It brings an encouraging environment that provides room to connect with others with similar goals and skills.

6 Thursday

Your patience and perseverance draw rewards. It connects you with an enterprising path that brings a prosperous sky overhead. It speaks of an opportunity that represents a windfall. It's a boost to your career path. You set sail on a voyage of developing your working life. It does let you chart a course forward towards success. This opportunity for growth breaks up stagnant energy patterns. It lifts the lid on a dynamic chapter.

7 Friday

A social aspect lightens the atmosphere. There is a focus on connecting with friends and family as life takes on a refreshing tone. It highlights communication and news as essential factor that draws sustenance and abundance into your world. You share thoughts and insights with someone who offers a refreshing perspective. Something you have been hoping for materializes soon, paving the way towards a lively environment.

8 Saturday

Your life heads on an upswing. It does bring a social aspect that paves the way forward with refreshing communication. There is a beautiful opportunity to improve your personal life. It brings expansion and spotlights a journey of growth and adventure. It is a balancing act between nurturing your romantic life and focusing on the functional areas that can appear humdrum but improves closeness.

9 Sunday ~ Mercury trine Neptune 23:56

Mercury in trine with Neptune focuses on your dreams and goals; it adds mental clarity that helps you stay focused as you work towards realizing your vision. Something you hope to reach in your life can reach fruition with the correct planning, adjustments, and focus. Creating space to nurture your priorities lets you reap the rewards of a dedicated approach that offers an increasing success rate.

10 Monday ~ Last Quarter Moon in Aries 1:48, Mars ingress Virgo 11:34, Mercury opposed Pluto 20:47

As the pace gathers momentum, you attract positive outcomes by maintaining a positive outlook on life. Committing to a course of action brings remarkable growth into your life. It sees motivation returning full force as you focus on developing unique goals that spark your interest. You invest time and energy into a journey that cultivates growth and well-being.

11 Tuesday ~ Mercury ingress Leo 4:09

You can stake your claim on improving your life as good fortune flows into your surroundings. Something special makes a grand entrance, which offers a treasure trove of possibilities. It has you thinking about making practical changes as you see progress and tangible results from your work to improve your life. You enter a time of working with your talents and nurturing your abilities. New leads emerge that crack the code to a wide-open road of potential.

12 Wednesday

Big news arrives soon, opening a cycle of growth for your life. It syncs up with a goal you've had in mind for some time. Exploring leads brings an enterprising approach that grows the path. You unearth a diamond in the rough that brings a purposeful and optimistic chapter into your life. Reawakening the creativity within your spirit brings rising confidence and renewed motivation. Staying adaptable lets you pivot at a moment's notice to capture a golden opportunity.

13 Thursday

News arrives to get an uptick of potential. It points you towards a happier journey that leaves struggles behind as you head towards a promising aspect that has you feeling inspired. Significant changes ahead bring good luck into your life. It takes you to a radiant time that offers blessings as you share with kindred spirits who offer thoughtful discussions. Nurturing your social life draws dividends as it helps you break fresh ground.

14 Friday ~ Sun sextile Uranus 23:02

In sextile with the Sun, Uranus captures the essence of surprises, new information, and discoveries. Something new and exciting is ready to manifest in your life. Being open to new people and possibilities charts a course towards rising prospects. It brings lighter energy that offers a refreshing element that nurtures harmony in your life. You soon transition to a path that provides an uptick of potential.

15 Saturday

An upbeat vibe works wonders for your self-esteem and confidence. It brings a social aspect that sees you spending more time with friends and kindred spirits. Enjoyable meetings and invitations to connect blossom, drawing happiness and expansion. Sharing with others brings a boost, and as morale rises, you discover new pathways tempting you forward. It brings romantic possibilities and a lighter influence.

16 Sunday

Making yourself a priority nurtures your life and opens your world to extraordinary growth. A fresh cycle beckons; it opens pathways of social connection and expansion. Your willingness to be open to meeting new people draws a pleasing result. A landscape of green and lush possibilities weaves magic around your future dreams. Entertaining discussions offer a lively and engaging time that encourages happiness.

17 Monday ~ Mercury square Jupiter 12:48, New Moon in Cancer 18:32

You direct your attention to a journey that advances your talents and refines your abilities. Working on your plan for the future gets everything ready to launch. Making tweaks and refinements is instrumental in drawing the best results possible. Your flexibility and creativity are valuable tools that help you chart a course toward achieving your dreams. New options offer a rising aspect that nurtures your life on many levels.

18 Tuesday ~ Islamic New Year

The past has been an extraordinary time that has grown your spirit remarkably. Taking time to rebalance your energy and focus on planning the path draws stability and grounded foundations. It gives you time to think and decide what project is best for your life. Creating the stepping stones clarifies what is essential and helps you launch forward effectively when the time is right for advancement.

19 Wednesday

You soon enter a landmark time of growth and progress. Information arrives and opens a path that fosters positive change. It connects you with a flow of possibilities that support expensively growing your life. It creates opportunities to mingle that broaden your circle of friends. Sharing with others sets an inspiring tone, allowing space to renew and restore positivity. Relationships improve as creating stronger foundations blossom into a path forward.

20 Thursday ~ Sun trine Neptune 13:06, Mars opposed Saturn 20:39

The Sun trine Neptune alignment raises the vibration around your life. It focuses on improving the circumstances in your life and helping others who face difficult circumstances. Creativity is a valuable resource that lets you craft plans that offer tangible impacts that enhance your world. Life brings essential changes that help you move away from outworn areas and embrace a more progressive path forward.

21 Friday

Something special makes a grand entrance and brings a chance to catch up with friends. An impromptu get-together draws a sparkling environment that promotes conversation, laughter, and kinship. It opens an optimistic time for sharing ideas with kindred spirits, and these discussions light up pathways of inspiration and creativity. It rekindles well-being and happiness and enables you to engage with a broader world of potential around your life.

22 Saturday ~ Sun opposed Pluto 3:52

The Sun shines a light on a hidden aspect Pluto keeps out of sight in your day-to-day life. This opposition Pluto creates a doorway through which pockets of the inner self, spirit, and primal energy can reach the surface of your awareness. It shines a light on subconscious desires and instincts. Life has an edgier aspect that can feel unsettling today. It does get you in touch with hidden depths that spark an internal dialogue as you reveal a personal element of your personality.

23 Sunday ~ Venus turns Retrograde in Leo 1:33, Sun ingress Leo 1:47

Venus turns retrograde, which slows the progress down around your love life. Romantic development slows down or stagnates during this phase. Focus on the building blocks as the journey is as important as the final destination. Avoid repeating limiting past patterns and walk a path that grows your life. An experimental flavor takes you towards developing your life. It sets a refreshing change of pace that fosters supportive conversations.

24 Monday

The wheels are in motion to attract unique options. You are transitioning towards significant life events that offer enhancements and improve the building blocks of your situation on a fundamental level. Being open to opportunities lets you transition to a landscape that helps you build an excellent foundation as you draw new prospects. Indeed, life favorably aligns to create an expressive and creative gateway forward.

25 Tuesday ~ First Quarter Moon in Libra 22:06

The seeds you nurture grow into a positive journey that promotes developing your talents and sharing your gifts with others. It connects you with a broader world of potential. Staying true to your desires, core values, and needs enables you to tap into your deep emotional awareness and be in tune with the person you are becoming. You enjoy feelings of stability, happiness, and contentment. It sees improvements in your life that develop goals centered around your heart.

26 Wednesday

Being open to new approaches helps you solve the riddle of improving your circumstances. Moving away from areas that no longer serve your higher purpose bring a renewed sense of hope into your life. A flash of insight cuts through the haze and helps you find the solutions needed to improve your circumstances. You emerge wiser and more resilient from a challenging chapter in your life.

27 Thursday ~ Mercury conjunct Venus 15:15

The Mercury conjunct Venus aspect today bodes well for your personal life. Communication flows, as does feelings, emotions, and sentiments. The time is right to share loving thoughts and receive positive feedback from someone who holds meaning in your life. Sharing ideas is instrumental in gaining insight into the path ahead. It gets you in the mood for expansion and growth as a new approach draws a pleasing result for your love life.

28 Friday ~ Delta Aquarids Meteor Shower. July 12th – August 23rd,
Mercury ingress Virgo 21:29

You can embrace the good fortune ahead as new options arrive. It lets you make a move towards improving your home life. It brings a supportive and engaging time to share ideas with friends. Gathering your resources, you get involved in an active and dynamic environment. It helps you plot a course towards improving circumstances.

29 Saturday

Nurturing your dreams draws a valuable result. There is a surprise nestled ahead that promotes social engagement. It leads to developments and new potential around your life that fosters an engaging journey of social involvement. Indeed, connecting with friends offers a wellspring of happiness and earmarks a time of growth in your life. It brings a chance to collaborate, which draws a valuable sense of support and kinship.

30 Sunday

News arrives, which enables you to plot a course towards greater security in your life. It brings improvement to your home and living situation. The floodgates of potential are opening, raising creativity, and bringing innovative solutions that nurture progress. Life improves through your willingness to work on the nuts and bolts of daily goals. Laying the groundwork enables you to develop plans sustainably.

AUGUST

Sun	Mon	Tue	Wed	Thu	Fri	Sat
		1	2	3	4	5
6	7	8	9	10	11	12
13	14	15	16	17	18	19
20	21	22	23	24	25	26
27	28	29	30	31		

New Moon

STURGEON MOON

31 Monday

Information arrives that opens the gate to an uptick of potential in your life. It brings new pathways that offer growth as you get a glimpse of a prestigious area that comes calling to advance life forward. Positive results help you feel confident and ready to tackle new goals enthusiastically. Acting on instincts lets you spot a diamond in the rough. This sideline project advances your skills and nurtures your abilities by refining and expanding your knowledge base.

1 Tuesday ~ Lammas/Lughnasadh, Super Moon,
Sturgeon Full Moon in Aquarius 18:32, Mars trine Jupiter 20:44

A nurturing chapter ahead connects with a sense of rejuvenation and renewal. It provides stable foundations that draw balance and security. As old challenges melt away, you open the door to a particular time of growing your life remarkably. New ideas provide sustenance and inspiration, and using your talents opens a wellspring of possibilities that leave you feeling optimistic.

2 Wednesday ~ Mercury opposed Saturn 2:16

As Mercury opposes Saturn, it brings heavy vibes into your life. The air of tension leaves a palpable sense of negativity around conversations and communication today. A serious-minded person may seek to have a strongly worded conversation with you. Setting boundaries and creating space to nurture the foundations in your life helps restore balance if talks become pessimistic today. Pushing business decisions off for another day is advisable.

3 Thursday

Exploring various leads for your life helps you discover a pathway that takes your talents toward an enterprising area. It brings a gift of stability that lets you focus on developing your goals. Something new blossoms in your life and helps you advance your abilities. Removing the doubt broadens your perception and opens the door to growth. Life moves forward with a strong emphasis on growing goals and developing your vision.

4 Friday

You uncover valuable information that offers a social aspect. It creates a stable environment for connecting with others as you share ideas. Weaving a web of connectedness in your social life gives you a leg up to a happier chapter. It encourages an expansive landscape that stimulates engaging conversations and creative ideas. It fosters a supportive vibe that nurtures grounded foundations. Opportunities to connect with friends bring optimism, drive, and happiness.

5 Saturday

Life picks up the pace and becomes more active and engaging. It lets you slip into a season of growth and expansion for your social life. Confidence rises and lights a path towards developing companionship. An influx of communication triggers an invitation to mingle. It connects you with sharing thoughts and ideas with friends who understand your personality and get your way of thinking. A self-expressive chapter ahead brings fun and friendship.

6 Sunday

Life becomes a blaze of new potential soon. Events line up to nourish your soul and nurture well-being in your life. Your willingness to work toward your dreams opens up an abundant landscape that lets you create remarkable progress. The way forward becomes bright and optimistic as you get a chance to rejuvenate life and nurture a wellspring of possibility. It brings a journey of self-development that lets you touch an ample time of growing dreams.

7 Monday ~ Sun square Jupiter 12:03

Today's Sun square Jupiter aspect raises confidence and brings good fortune swirling around your life. It does boost your ego, which could lead to you overstepping the mark. Knowing your capabilities and working within the systems you have in place for your life will help keep things in check during this energetic time. Life is ripe with potential and ready to blossom. You breeze through an ample time of discovering new possibilities.

8 Tuesday ~ Last Quarter Moon in Taurus 10:48

Researching various options helps you develop a winning trajectory. It draws a lighter path that offers a learning curve you find fascinating. A new role grows your skills, and your attention to detail and meticulous approach develop your talents. It brings a productive chapter that heightens security in your life. Gaining traction on your working goals helps you create substantial gains that improve your day-to-day life.

9 Wednesday ~ Venus square Uranus 11:09

A surprise element adds a sense of intrigue to your personal/social life due to the Venus square Uranus aspect today. Unexpected developments bring a happy surprise into your life. It orients you towards growing your social life and brings a time of engagement and fun into your world. It gets warm and enriching moments that provide substantial benefits as you link up with others who support your world.

10 Thursday ~ Mercury at Greatest Elongation 27.4 E, Mercury trine Jupiter 12:45

Mercury trine Jupiter today brings a boost to your life. Jupiter is the planet of good luck and fortuitous happenings, which improves the potential possible around your circumstances. A surprise crops up that lets the tides turn in your favor. It carries information that bolsters your mood and emphasizes growing your life outwardly. It links up to a productive time that lets you cast your net wide and come up with lots of opportunities worth developing.

11 Friday

You soon get your bearings in a unique landscape of potential. It connects your life with an area worth growing. An undercurrent of change draws new adventures that offer liberation and expansion into your life. A big reveal draws a sense of celebration and excitement as you connect with inspiration and unearth the right path forward for your life. It soon triggers rising prospects in your social life that cultivate an abundant landscape of potential.

12 Saturday ~ Perseids Meteor Shower July 17th - Aug 24th

New possibilities heighten the potential in your life. It opens a social aspect that connects you with others who resonate on the same wavelength. Nurturing communication facilitates growth as an invitation arrives, which creates a flurry of excitement. It helps you kick off an engaging time of expansion and sharing. You open the door to explore a wide vista of refreshing potential around your social life.

13 Sunday

News arrives that unlocks a happier chapter in your life. It brings communication that promotes growth in your social life. You discover you can develop life and create a bridge to a brighter path. It opens a journey that facilitates meeting companions as you get busy expanding your horizons. A positive trend brings a boost as it opens the gate to sharing with others. A social environment connects you with a busy time that opens a way forward.

14 Monday

Information arrives that opens the gate to a prosperous time of developing your talents. Exploring various avenues for your working life blends beautifully with this news. It enables you to advance your core skills and elevate the potential around your life. Developing your career brings heightened security into view, which promotes stable and grounded foundations in your life. Surging possibilities fuel inspiration to grow your options.

15 Tuesday

News arrives that links you up with rising prospects. It opens an enterprising time for developing your goals. Working with your talents and sharing thoughts and ideas with kindred spirits brings a growing journey that offers advancement. It draws collaboration and the possibility of getting involved with a group endeavor. It marks a time of get-togethers shared with friends as sunny skies breeze into your life, offering a positive influence.

16 Wednesday ~ Sun square Uranus 2:34, New Moon in Leo 09:37, Mars trine Uranus 13:53

Uranus steals the show today, and you can expect a spontaneous and expressive environment that offers a breath of fresh air in your life. It does set the tone for an ambitious time of progressing your dreams. It lays the correct groundwork that paves the way toward an inspirational chapter. Information arrives out of the blue and provides you with a unique opportunity.

17 Thursday

Fundamental changes bring a shift forward that offers new opportunities for your life. It opens a journey that promotes developing friendships, bringing more security on offer in your social life. It shines a light on a short refreshing time of lively conversations that open the gateway towards a happy environment. Information arrives that promotes social engagement and sharing with your tribe.

18 Friday

A positive influence brings unique options to your table. You can break free of limitations and expand life outwardly as news arrives that culminates in a happy occasion. Indeed, an invitation ahead offers a social aspect that clears the path forward in your life. It brings a time of mingling with kindred spirits, and this networking places you in the box seat to form a new friendship as you broaden your circle of connections.

19 Saturday

Changes arrive that sweep fresh air into your surroundings. It brings an opportunity that is meant specifically for your attention. Consequently, it earmarks new leads that help you obtain progress and results. A clear path opens, which may make you take the road less traveled. You find people entering your life soon, which happens for a reason. It brings a journey that has you feeling on track to develop your circle of friends.

20 Sunday

The seeds you plant blossom into a path of busyness. An enterprising chapter of growth is ahead. It takes you towards developing your vision per your goals. Life blesses you on many levels when communication arrives out of the blue. It lets you clear the decks for a happy and social chapter. Your circumstances are evolving; it brings positive influences that offer a chance to expand your horizons into new areas.

21 Monday

There is a lot of potential surrounding your life; it brings the ideal moment to take the plunge and develop your dreams in a new area. A project you create begins to take shape, which connects you with more significant expansion that increases stability and security in your life. You move forward toward a remarkable trajectory of growth and advancement. Developing your abilities and nurturing your skills cracks the code to a robust phase of rising prospects.

22 Tuesday ~ Venus square Jupiter 12:13, Mars opposed Neptune 20:33

A Venus Jupiter square offers rising prospects for your love life. You will have trouble concentrating on the task as fun moments capture your attention. A lovely change enables you to nurture more personal aspects. An area you seek to develop brings enriching and meaningful prospects into your life. You feel that life has more substance and significance as you concentrate on goals that hold the most significant meaning around your situation.

23 Wednesday ~ Sun ingress Virgo 8:58, Mercury turns retrograde 19:59

Mercury turns retrograde and puts a damper on the potential possible in your social life. It can cause miscommunication and issues in your love life. Mercury in retrograde adds an element that turns communication haywire. It disrupts the positive flow of energy in your life. Delay signing contracts or committing to business deals during a retrograde phase. It is appropriate to plan and launch new endeavors after the retrograde cycle.

24 Thursday ~ First Quarter Moon in Sagittarius 9:57

You reveal the news that cracks the code to advance your skills. You enter a new cycle of growth that helps you grow and prosper as you develop your abilities. It links to positive change that lays the groundwork to build a stable foundation in your life. Being adaptable and open to change helps you advance your talents into a unique area that excitingly expands your life. Research and planning are valuable tools to unearth the right leads.

25 Friday ~ Mars trine Pluto 12:22

Today's aspect offers rising prospects for your career. It brings a goal-orientated, disciplined, and centered focus on improving your working life. Finding your groove and adopting a middle path forward nurtures greater security and grounded foundations. You discover you can advance considerably by growing your goals sustainably and moderately. Cultivating tranquillity and balance helps you achieve remarkable outcomes.

26 Saturday

There will be important developments around your life; taking a closer look at the potential possible helps you unearth the right direction. You are ready for change, and a new chapter doesn't disappoint when it offers a trailblazing path forward. You hit your peak stride as you cultivate happiness and expansion in your social life. Life gathers momentum, bringing a vibrant landscape that draws a boost. Thoughtful conversations blaze a trail towards enriching life.

27 Sunday ~ Sun opposed Saturn 8:28, Mars ingress Libra r 13:15

Nurturing the foundations in your life draws a balanced and abundant landscape. It is natural and reasonable to feel anxious as you deal with uncertainties in your life. Focusing on the basics and nurturing your home life draws a solid foundation to grow your world. A new approach ahead draws lightness and happiness into your life. It connects you with companions who support and nurture your world. Sharing discussions facilitates harmony.

28 Monday

Remarkable opportunities for growth soon land in your lap. Expanding your life and nurturing your abilities fortifies the foundations in your world. You connect with a unique crew of characters who grow your circle of friends. It offers trailblazing brainstorming times shared with kindred spirits who light up pathways of inspiration and creativity. A joint project or collaboration is earmarked for your life and becomes a source of pride.

29 Tuesday ~ Uranus turns Retrograde in Taurus 2:11

Uranus moving into a retrograde phase boosts idealism; it offers big sky pictures that help motivate change to improve the world around you. This planetary cycle will boost your confidence and foster leadership qualities. It deepens initiative and offers a fresh wind that spurs creativity. It cultivates an impressive journey that takes you towards greener pastures. A course or other learning possibility helps break down barriers and leads towards growth.

30 Wednesday

Good energy flows easily and naturally into your world as you reveal exciting options which offer a buzz of excitement. It underscores a time of change ahead in your life that helps things fall into place. Letting go of fixed expectations helps you move beyond areas that limit progress. You create space for unique possibilities to emerge and grow your life. Expanding horizons allows you to establish your talents in a forward-facing direction.

31 Thursday ~ Super Moon, Blue Full Moon in Pisces 1:36

This Full Moon represents transformation in your life. It signifies cutting away from areas that limit progress and heading towards change. It can feel disruptive in the short term as a sense of chaos can cloud the path ahead. Taking a step back from sensitive areas provides a broader perspective that nourishes a healing influence. Removing the outworn energy resolves sensitive areas and helps you move towards greener pastures.

SEPTEMBER

Sun	Mon	Tue	Wed	Thu	Fri	Sat
					1	2
3	4	5	6	7	8	9
10	11	12	13	14	15	16
17	18	19	20	21	22	23
24	25	26	27	28	29	30

New Moon

CORN/HARVEST MOON

1 Friday

Some lovely changes emerge, which help promote a growth-orientated phase in your life. It enables you to blaze a pioneering trail toward developing your dreams. It lays the groundwork for growing your world outwardly as an uptick of options ahead sees inspiration surging. It offers room to mingle with friends, facilitating blending ideas with others who provide thoughtful discussions.

2 Saturday

A more prosperous life experience emerges as communication arrives to bring a boost into your life. It helps you find a groove with friends and companions who support your life. It brings courageous conversations that land new ideas tinged with fresh inspiration. You enter an enriching time that promotes warm conversations and engaging moments. Constructive dialogues place a spotlight on developing shared goals.

3 Sunday

It is a time that binds you to your home environment. It brings a positive trend that moves towards stabilizing foundations and restoring equilibrium. It helps you take advantage of opportunities that offer impressive personal growth. Developing passions brings inspiration. Life becomes smoother as you untangle the knots that disrupt your energy. It provides a bold self-made flavor; you may begin researching a new project.

4 Monday ~ Labor Day, Venus turns direct in Leo 1:19,
Mercury trine Jupiter 10:29, Jupiter turns Retrograde in Taurus 14:14

Venus turns direct and brings an open road of potential into your love life. A new cycle emerges for your love life and brings a welcome boost to your spirit. A strong emphasis on improving your circumstances draws a pleasing result. It offers a journey of self-improvement and creativity. It lifts the lid on an enriching chapter in your life.

5 Tuesday

The beneficial changes ahead allow you to prove your abilities and talents. It is a testing ground that challenges you on many levels. It does bring advancement, and this refines your skills. You may be learning a new and unfamiliar path that grows your world. It does create actual progress that brings a solid foundation from which to build the way ahead. It is a time when you live primarily and enjoy the rewards of your labor.

6 Wednesday ~ Sun conjunct Mercury 11: 08, Last Quarter Moon in Gemini 22:21

Independent thinking and innovative ideas can be attributed to the Sun and Mercury conjunct today. Fortune aligns to form a clear window of opportunity that expands life forward. Progression is surprisingly swift as advancement comes calling. Plotting a course towards developing new goals fosters enriching moments. Staying open to new options brings an enterprise that feeds your creativity and grows your talents.

7 Thursday

You have a firm goal in mind, which is beneficial as it sets the tone for your vision. You have gifts of perseverance and determination. While you have experienced setbacks, you can stay tuned as new growth and opportunities soon drive a goal home. The difficulties of the past become a distant memory. Honing in on your real purpose brings happiness and draws abundance. It fires up a collaboration with someone significant as you head towards entering a happier chapter.

8 Friday ~ Sun trine Jupiter 11:12

The Sun forms a trine with Jupiter, which increases good luck and fortune in your life. A positive influence nurtures beneficial outcomes as news arrives that lifts the lid on a promising chapter. It seals the deal on promoting your social life. Taking full advantage of the opportunities ahead brings a productive and full schedule to light the way forward. It points towards a happy chapter that lets you leave struggles behind in the rear vision mirror.

9 Saturday

The changes ahead bring freedom and expansion. Seeking out new adventures connects you with your broader social circle. It does get a dynamic and continuously evolving chapter of potential. An experimental flavor brings moments to treasure with friends and companions. It fuels your motivation with inspiration. It lets you overcome the barriers of the mind and confidently chase your dreams.

10 Sunday

The attractive options ahead leave you feeling optimistic. It opens a time that brings changes to your social life. Getting involved with sharing with friends opens an engaging and fascinating chapter. It brings stabilizing energy that heightens well-being and lights a path toward developing joint projects. Transformation and rejuvenation resonate around your life. It does highlight new options that encourage you to expand your horizons.

11 Monday

News arrives that brings a sense of providence into your life. It opens a journey of new horizons and possibilities. It helps you launch towards a meaningful area that sparks movement and discovery. It brings a time of developing leads and mapping out a strategy for future contingencies. A curious path comes calling and offers to advance your skills to the next level. It forms the basis of a grounded chapter that progresses life forward.

12 Tuesday

You can expect new options to emerge soon. It shifts your focus towards developing an enterprising area that grows your skills. It is the continuation of a more comprehensive change theme that emphasizes developing knowledge and remarkably increasing your life. It takes you to a radiant time of designing your creativity and working with your skills to effect positive results. A shift forward brings a lovely boost to your world.

13 Wednesday

Life supports your efforts to improve circumstances. New possibilities spark a journey that offers expansion. It shines a light on goals, status, and career success. Putting the finishing touches on your strategy lets you develop a winning trajectory when news arrives that encourages expansion. Rising prospects open up an avenue that offers growth and security. It allows you to move towards advancement.

14 Thursday

A turning point occurs that offers advancement for your working life. It lets you dive into uncharted territory and discover growth is possible when you push against the barriers of perceived expectations. An opportunity ahead fosters rising optimism. You get involved in learning an area that holds water and revs up the success rate for your career. As you create a bridge towards growing your dreams, you discover a venture that opens the door wide.

15 Friday ~ Rosh Hashanah (begins at sunset), New Moon in Virgo 1:40, Mercury turns direct at 20:20

Mercury turns direct, and this improves communication and interpersonal bonds. It offers a renewed interest in your social life that helps harmonize the frazzled tensions during the retrograde phase. Opportunity knocks, giving you a sign that things are shifting forward. It heralds an end of difficulties, allowing you to achieve closure on a difficult phase; you turn the page on a fresh chapter.

16 Saturday ~ Sun trine Uranus 1:23

Today, the Sun trine Uranus aspect adds a dash of spontaneity and excitement into your life. It is a favorable aspect that brings the freedom-driven chapter to light. Focusing on your social life draws a pleasing result as you connect with folk who offer excitement and passion. Thoughtful discussions attract unique ideas that spark a refreshing time shared with kindred spirits. Being open to new people and possibilities draws a pleasing result for your social life.

17 Sunday ~ Rosh Hashanah (ends at sunset), Venus square Jupiter 6:12

The Venus square Jupiter aspect makes it the perfect day for unwinding and relaxing with your social circle. An easygoing vibe draws thoughtful conversations and entertaining ideas. News arrives to bring an uptick of potential into your family life. It directs your attention to nurturing home and family foundations. It brings steady progress that boosts interpersonal bonds and family ties.

18 Monday

As you merge your dreams and hopes with the rising tide of refreshing options, life goes your way. Developing your abilities kicks off an enterprising chapter of personal growth ahead. A prominent area comes calling, bringing the exciting potential to the surface. It redefines your journey ahead and broadens the scope of what you thought was possible in your world. Climbing the ladder towards success brings a steady progression.

19 Tuesday ~ Sun opposed Neptune 11:17

Your perception broadens as the Sun lights up Neptune's dreamy aspects. Engaging with creativity and imagination draws rising ideas and innovative concepts to consider. Being open to change and possibilities lets you move forward towards developing new goals. There is a beautiful symmetry in the coming chapter that offers renewal and healing while enabling you to grow your life in a unique journey forward.

20 Wednesday

Opening your life to new possibilities brings an active environment ahead. Expanding the borders of your world brings a pleasing result that nurtures a more creative and expressive tone. Working with your talents and leaning into your strengths helps shape your goals and create the right environment from which to blossom. It triggers an active phase of movement and discovery that positions you to increase the potential in your life and head towards prosperity.

21 Thursday ~ International Day of Peace, Sun trine Pluto 5:20

Browsing options for development sparks an emotional journey that grows your vision in a new direction. It links up with information that arrives in a flurry of excitement. A large part of this news focuses on self-development and prioritizing your goals. You score a lucrative avenue that offers rising prospects and a secure basis from which to grow your world. Being resourceful and researching new options brings a pleasing result that offers advancement.

22 Friday ~ Sun ingress Libra 6:46, First Quarter Moon in Sagittarius 19:32, Mercury at Greatest Elongation 17.9W

You open the floodgates to a lucky chapter as the changes ahead clear the deck for the new potential to flourish in your world. An area you pour your energy into it is productive and rewarding. Setting your intentions creates potent alchemy that adds magic and inspiration to your ideas. Being proactive draws dividends as improvements swiftly follow the expansion of horizons.

23 Saturday ~ Mabon/Fall Equinox 6:50

It is a terrific time that offers a chance to renew and rebuild your lifestyle. It highlights the fine things in life that hold the most significant meaning. Something on offer welcomes a productive phase. The information ahead guides your objectives forward. It facilitates growth and leads to heightened security. Grounded and enriching energy flows into your world, strengthening close personal bonds.

24 Sunday ~ Yom Kippur (begins at sunset)

You benefit from developments on the horizon as bright news draws blessings into your life. It brings a busy time that helps you build stable foundations as you nurture new possibilities that inspire growth in your world. It brings a time of exchanging thoughts with kindred spirits as you chart a course towards expanding your circle of friends. Sharing with others offer rejuvenation and is food for your soul.

25 Monday ~ Yom Kippur (ends at sunset), Mercury trine Jupiter 12:12

Today's Mercury trine Jupiter aspect brings optimism and good news. Research, learning, study, and socializing are favored. This trine is ideal for formulating new plans and engaging in future-orientated brainstorming sessions. It's also the perfect time to sort and organize; your office, workspace, closet, or even your whole life. Making effective changes takes productivity to the next level.

26 Tuesday

You reveal a clue that gives you insight into the path ahead. Life heads to an upswing, bringing news of a new role that develops your abilities and takes you towards advancement. Working with your skills opens the road to an impressive time of deepening your knowledge. It sparks a journey that leaves you optimistic about your life's prospects. Friends play a role in developing the journey ahead. Firing creativity lets you strike gold and turn the corner on a winning chapter.

27 Wednesday

Changes ahead enable you to cultivate magic and possibility. Many new options will help you turn a corner and grow life in a new direction. Creativity and inspiration surge in your world as you hone in on a higher sense of purpose. It imbues a sweeter flavor that adds the right taste of success. It has you thinking about the future from a new perspective. A creative undertaking you become involved with developing soon takes shape.

28 Thursday

You benefit from developments on the horizon. It brings blessings as you head towards a productive chapter that is lively and dynamic. It leaves you feeling optimistic about the future. New inspiration sweeps into your life that clears the path forward. Life expands as you draw profitable opportunities that focus on improving your circumstances. It does let you embrace life-affirming endeavors that stabilize and bring balance into your environment.

OCTOBER

Sun	Mon	Tue	Wed	Thu	Fri	Sat
1	2	3	4	5	6	7
8	9	10	11	12	13	14
15	16	17	18	19	20	21
22	23	24	25	26	27	28
29	30	31				

New Moon

Hunters Moon

**29 Friday ~ Sukkot (begins at sunset), Super Moon, Corn Moon,
Harvest Full Moon in Aries 9:58, Venus square Uranus 17:53**

A restless vibe caused by a Venus Uranus square could undermine the security in your love life or the broader social environment if you are single. A freedom-loving vibration brings a need to be spontaneous and engage in unique adventures that change the day-to-day routine of your life. The changes ahead encourage the expansion of your social life.

30 Saturday ~Mercury trine Uranus 16:56

Today's trine is perfect for using technology to keep life supported and flowing in your social life. Communication is your passageway to a more active social life. Being innovative and thinking outside the box connects you with diverse pathways of growth and expansion. As your social environment becomes more connected, it establishes a grounded foundation to draw balance and happiness into your life.

1 Sunday

A blended approach with another person initiates a new beginning. It offers progression and brings inspiration flowing into your world. It marks the start of a productive chapter that lets you chase your passion. It brings an improvement of stability to your home front. A compelling journey awaits your open heart and mind. An area you focus on gets the green light to move forward, and you can appreciate a lucky break.

2 Monday ~ Mercury opposed Neptune 3:34

The Mercury and Neptune opposition helps you communicate your ideas and thoughts today. However, You may find work challenging as rising creativity brings a desire to daydream. You discover the right path and soon can head for your dreams. Laying groundwork does secure foundations that are grounded. It creates the perfect basis from which to grow your future life. Rising prospects ahead help you clear the slate and open a new road of potential in your life.

3 Tuesday ~ Mercury trine Pluto 19:20

New possibilities light a fire under your inspiration soon. You make good progress on developing a goal. It sparks a journey that offers pearls of wisdom. It does have you feeling optimistic about the prospects ahead. The wayside flings limitations aside as you enter this transformational chapter of growth. It lights a path of inspiration and creativity; it has you expanding your options into new areas. It brings a time to increase your abilities and shine your talents.

4 Wednesday

A surge of optimism opens the window to a bright chapter in your life. It brings a more vibrant environment that offers an enterprising time of growth and progress. Improvement in your circumstances becomes a strong focus as you push past barriers and head towards gold. It brings a winning chapter of nurturing life and developing your talents. Pouring your energy into creating a significant area brings joy.

5 Thursday ~ Mercury ingress Libra 12:06

Mercury can bring an indecisive vibe that causes stagnant energy. Procrastination can be an issue that delays progress in the workplace. Removing distractions and streamlining your environment can help mitigate the effect of this transit. The biggest obstacles are your limitations; fostering a proactive mindset removes the roadblocks. News arrives, which brings a boost to your life.

6 Friday ~ Sukkot (ends at sunset), Last Quarter Moon in Cancer 13:48

Things are on the move when communication arrives that helps you create headway around developing a more prosperous social life. Life aligns favorably as an invitation to mingle brings harmony to the top of your world. It launches a time of sharing thoughtful discussions and building balance foundations. Focusing on the areas that hold the most significant promise helps revamp your situation as you head towards an abundant landscape of possibility.

7 Saturday ~ Draconids Meteor Shower. Oct 6-10

News arrives that brings a boost. It offers a new project with a strong focus on working with your talents. Dabbling in a creative interest helps make the most of your capabilities as your talents shine when keeping busy. It offers a purposeful and inspiring path that cultivates your skills and advances life. You reveal hidden depths of insight that enable progress to occur. Removing the confusion allows for a unique journey to blossom.

8 Sunday

Nurturing your home life brings notable changes that offer a path of growth and progression. It translates to a new chapter of possibility that promotes interpersonal bonds and brings a relaxed ambiance and thoughtful discussions to the forefront of your life. It jumpstarts an active time of open communication that improves the foundations of your life. It brings an engaging time that feels good for your soul.

9 Monday ~ Thanksgiving Day (Canada), Indigenous People's Day, Columbus Day, Mars square Pluto 1:04, Venus ingress Virgo 1:06

An insightful person shares advice and voices their thoughts with you. It brings a sense of support and an opportunity for collaboration with this person. You soon ease into a busy and productive time of developing your abilities and working with your talents as you grow your vision for the future. Extending your reach into a new area brings possibilities that nurture change in your world.

10 Tuesday ~ Venus opposed Saturn at 6:11. Pluto turns direct at 11:43

As life heads towards an upward trajectory, you land in an environment ripe with possibilities. You set sail on a timely voyage that expands your life outwardly. Nurturing your life hits a sweet spot that draws abundance into your world. A situation you invest time and energy into blossoms into a path forward. It ushers in a more connected and supportive environment. It sets the stage for an expressive and happy time ahead.

11 Wednesday

Taking full advantage of the opportunities ahead brings a productive and full schedule. A flurry of activity has you feeling valued and appreciated. Life brings new assignments and projects that are useful in establishing a grounded and balanced environment. New prospects bubble up to keep your creative energy sparking. Significant changes ahead draw good fortune into your world. It brings sunnier skies as you take on new assignments that showcase your skills.

12 Thursday ~ Mars ingress Scorpio 3:59

You scale new heights and reach for a lofty goal. It brings a time of working with your skills and evolving your talents as you take on a learning course and cultivate more significant opportunities for your life. A new financial or career option appears and brings rising prospects into your life. It brings a journey of beginnings, opportunities, and potential. It provides expansion and progress as you soon crack the code to a brighter chapter that takes your abilities forward

13 Friday ~ Mars trine Saturn 12:28

The Mars trine Saturn aspect today boosts your working life. It enables you to gain traction on achieving a successful result. It puts the finishing touches on your working week as you easily meet deadlines. This robust transit gives you the strength, ambition, and perseverance to take on the most complex tasks and complete them on time. Increased productivity and efficiency get the job done. Your self-discipline keeps you focused without being distracted or discouraged.

14 Saturday ~ New Moon in Libra 17:54, Annular Solar Eclipse 17:59

New adventures come calling, which lets you broaden your reach and branch out into unique areas of interest. Through careful planning and concentrated effort, you achieve a pleasing result in your life. It brings a path of pure potentiality into your life. This abundant chapter is a journey that can be grown and developed. As you move forward, you connect with exceptional people and curious opportunities that continue to grow your life outwardly.

15 Sunday

Information arrives with positive news. There is an element of surprise in this message. It emphasizes your social and home life as you gain happy news and can get busy developing friendships. It improves your social life and brings you a chance to mingle with friends. New possibilities attract lively discussions that nurture creativity and fresh ideas. It opens the floodgates to a positive chapter that offers growth and well-being.

16 Monday

Information arrives that could bring an entrepreneurial direction. It lets you advance your interests into a new area. Focusing on preparing the path ahead draws progression. You enter a highly productive time that is ripe for expansion. You benefit from events on the horizon as they let you gather your resources while planning the strategy for next year. You take on an ambitious journey, but it draws joy.

17 Tuesday

Your creativity heightens and brings essential changes that draw a fresh start. You welcome a surge of new possibilities that bring an optimistic phase into your life. It is a time of expansion that begins the building blocks to a path of progress and plenty. Permitting yourself to chase your dreams is the first step forward. It lands you in an environment ripe with potential and ready to blossom.

18 Wednesday

Sharing experiences with another person gets a wellspring of harmony into your surroundings. It lets you gain traction on improving your circumstances. Progressing your vision forward brings a positive shift you can embrace. Advancement is looming, and this takes you to a diligent time building your dream. It takes your abilities to the next level and ignites a substantial growth phase.

19 Thursday

The goals you've been working towards finally reach a tipping point, bringing them to fruition and completion. It does have you thinking about the next major project for your life. Developing your knowledge and skill set gets you up to speed with advancing your life to the next level. It brings a group project that connects you with like-minded people. An exciting enterprise soon lands in your life.

20 Friday ~ Sun conjunct Mercury 5:37

In conjunction with Mercury, the Sun is a favorable aspect that attracts communication. It is the best of all elements for receiving or sending communication. Interacting with others is vital today. It stimulates your need to share ideas and engage in thoughtful discussions that nurture well-being and harmony in your life. You soon enter clear skies as new information lands to kick off a social aspect of your life.

21 Saturday ~ Orionids Meteor Shower Oct 2ⁿᵈ – Nov 7ᵗʰ,
Mercury square Pluto 12:50, Sun square Pluto 14:09

Today's aspect causes a challenging environment as you find your judgment or authority tested. Being challenged and tested feels uncomfortable as you think you are making the right choices and decisions for your life. The Mercury square Pluto transit also attracts interactions with other people who feed the gossip mill and cultivate drama, leading to a toxic environment.

22 Sunday ~ First Quarter Moon in Aquarius 03:29, Venus trine Jupiter 4:32,
Mercury ingress Scorpio 6:46, Mercury trine Saturn 16:12

The Venus trine Jupiter aspect offers golden threads around your social and love life. It is one of the most anticipated transits which harmonizes interpersonal bonds and offers rising prospects of good luck to your romantic life. It is fascinating to those seeking love or wanting a deeper romantic bond. Opportunities enable you to circulate with friends and attract good people.

23 Monday ~ Venus at Greatest Elongation 46.4W, Sun ingress Scorpio 16:17

Life moves from strength to strength. You are adept at achieving your vision through your willingness to navigate hurdles and come out on top. Your pioneering attitude draws dividends as it brings a venture that lets you use your talents significantly. You harness the essence of manifestation, allowing this potential to blossom. It enables you to settle into a productive groove that brings long-term growth into view.

24 Tuesday ~ Sun trine Saturn 7:13

Today's Sun, Saturn trine, gives you a commanding presence in the workplace. Confidence peaks in mid-afternoon, enabling you to effectively manage the day's tasks with relative ease as your energy keeps humming along productively. You conquer the workload and achieve a robust result with your consistent and disciplined efforts, which draw a pleasing effect and the added benefits of increased job satisfaction.

25 Wednesday

Your willingness to be flexible and open to change draws dividends. It helps you stay on top of your game and places you in the box seat to improve your circumstances. It smooths out the rollercoaster and takes you to a more balanced and stable environment. A new assignment emerges that is a good fit for your creativity. It brings a project that activates your talents and harnesses your creative side.

26 Thursday

A windfall lights a path of expansion. Intuition is a strong helper that guides your way during uncertain times. Your welcome new responsibilities and pathways towards developing your talents. Something you apply for is accepted, bringing a burst of excitement into your world. It lets you make impressive tracks towards developing your plans. Your work behind the scenes is instrumental in advancing your situation forward.

27 Friday

Getting involved with friends draws a pleasing result. It sparks an enriching journey towards developing companionship and mingling with kindred spirits. Rejuvenation and renewal nurture well-being in your life as you get involved with sharing and caring for friends. Mixing with your tribe reduces stress and supports a journey of healing and discovery. Something special is brewing in the background, creating a potent mix of potential in your life.

28 Saturday ~ Mars opposed Jupiter 16: 03, Hunters Full Moon in Taurus 20:23 Partial Lunar Eclipse 20:14

You can embrace one of the luckiest aspects today when Mars opposes Jupiter and draws good fortune into your life. The winds of change carry news information into your surroundings. Today's transit increases your self-confidence and ability to handle your time and energy demands. It brings a competitive edge that fuels ambitions and the desire to achieve your goals.

29 Sunday ~ Mercury opposed Jupiter 3:44, Mercury conjunct Mars 14:21

Today, Mercury is the show's star and draws a favorable aspect that nurtures good fortune in your social life. It brings a chance to share with friends and loved ones. Relaxing and unwinding enable you to restore frazzled nerves and build robust foundations. It connects you with a creative and insightful landscape that focuses on looking at your future goals. Lively discussions draw constructive dialogues that are perfect for brainstorming.

NOVEMBER

Sun	Mon	Tue	Wed	Thu	Fri	Sat
			1	2	3	4
5	6	7	8	9	10	11
12	13	14	15	16	17	18
19	20	21	22	23	24	25
26	27	28	29	30		

New Moon

Beaver Moon

30 Monday

Invitations arrive by surprise, and one message shines a light on excitement and adventure. It is a time that brings sudden, dynamic news. It brings a bond that offers a sense of connection and joy. It enriches your life and adds support where you need it the most. It brings an uplifting time that includes invitations to social events. It lets you step up into a more social and active environment. Time with valued companions charts a course towards a happy chapter.

31 Tuesday ~ Samhain/Halloween, All Hallows Eve Venus trine Uranus 12:51

Embrace a magical and vibrant Halloween under the influence of an engaging and dynamic Venus trine Uranus aspect that adds a dash of spontaneity and fun into your life. Under this positive influence, you enjoy a carefree time that ushers in lighter energy. It brings a shift forward that nurtures companionship and brings a lively time of chasing your vision. Positive sharing fosters engaging conversations that bring a connected environment into view.

1 Wednesday ~ All Saints' Day

You soon enter an enterprising chapter that brings change into your world. It offers a fresh start for your life that reveals new growth is ready to blossom. A positive trend ahead ushers in advancement as you begin learning an area that offers to grow your skills. Developing your talents unlocks pathways of growth that offer rising prospects for your life. An endeavor you focus your energy on developing offers room to advance your abilities to the next level.

2 Thursday

A whirlwind of activity opens an opportunity that supports learning and advancement. You make an intelligent decision regarding the development of your ideas. It brings an outlet for your restless energy that nurtures your spirit and creates a secure foundation from which to grow your world. It has you moving into unique territory as you advance your skills to the next level. New choices and opportunities attract excitement and spur inspiration to new levels.

3 Friday ~ Sun opposed Jupiter at 5:02. Venus opposed Neptune at 22:05

The Sun opposed to Jupiter, brings the increasing potential for wealth and good fortune. Rising prospects let you turn a corner and head towards a lucky streak. Information arrives soon, which is a game-changer for your social life. It does unleash fresh possibilities that improve your world. It kicks off a social and active environment that leads to engaging conversations. It opens a gateway toward personal growth and soon draws harmony into your surroundings.

4 Saturday ~ Taurids Meteor Shower. Sept 7th - Dec 10th
Saturn turns direct in Pisces at 7:15. Mercury opposed Uranus at 16:06

The Mercury opposed Uranus transit bringing a chaotic and hectic pace. The busier pace may leave you feeling tense, anxious, and scattered. Uranus adds an unexpected vibe, leaving you scrambling to deal with surprise news. Information emerges from the left field, leaving you wondering what will happen next. Focusing on the basics improves balance.

5 Sunday ~ Last Quarter Moon in Leo 08:37

Your positive outlook is instrumental in bringing new opportunities into your life. The tides turn in your favor as you enter an energizing time that broadens your circle of friends. It brings stable foundations into your life as you deepen a bond with someone who holds similar values and thoughts on life. It brings a sense of fun and excitement into your social life as you mingle with a refreshing character who offers lively sessions of sharing ideas.

6 Monday ~ Venus trine Pluto 14:38

Today's Venus trine with Pluto adds intensity to your love life. This aspect turns up the heat in your personal life. Sexual attraction and passion rise as you get busy developing your personal life. Singles will likely find new romance soon, while couples can embrace a more connected and sizzling love life. It drives a freedom-driven time that embraces the essence of adventure. It lets you let loose and open the gate to a happy chapter that hits an energizing note in your life.

7 Tuesday ~ Mercury trine Neptune 1:36

Creativity, imagination, and innovation blaze a wildfire of inspiration as Mercury and Neptune form a trine today. Increased sensitivity to this vibrational energy attracts a boost into your world that bolsters vitality. It offers a dramatic shift that helps you quickly learn or develop a new area. It draws a dynamic chapter that lets you unwrap benefits worth exploring. Something impressive flows into your field of vision.

8 Wednesday ~ Venus ingress Libra 9:27

A gateway ahead brings a journey of new adventures into your social life. Light-hearted discussions with diverse and quirky characters help you find your groove in an engaging environment. Opportunities to mingle and share thoughts with artistic companions spark creativity and usher fresh ideas to contemplate development. It is a time that brings terrific options to light and offers an enticing path toward achieving growth.

9 Thursday ~ Mercury sextile Pluto 12:16

Today, the Mercury sextile Pluto transit adds extra layers and dimensions to your creative thinking. It brings an ideal time for research, planning, and mapping out unique areas for future development. Your penetrating inquiries delve deep and help you discover potential pitfalls and issues. Your inquiring mind places you in a solid position to grow your dreams as you do due diligence and understand all aspects of your investigations.

10 Friday ~ Veterans Day (Observed), Mercury ingress Sagittarius 6:22, Mercury square Saturn 15:07

Today's Mercury square Saturn challenges critical thinking skills and intrepid enquiring. Tensions could flare up and lead to disruptions. Miscommunication is more likely when you are not on the same page as the person you talk to about your thoughts and ideas. Fostering a proactive mindset helps removes the roadblocks.

11 Saturday ~ Veterans Day, Remembrance Day (Canada), Mars opposed Uranus 21:11

The Mars opposed Uranus could catch you off guard today, leading to tension in personal bonds. An unexpected tension could flare up, causing an argument with a family member or loved one. Being understanding, flexible, and diplomatic goes far to help stabilize foundations. Blame it on Mars if tensions arise with friends or family. This energy soon shifts, creating a better landscape.

12 Sunday

Life brings essential changes which help you move away from adverse environments and embrace a more progressive aspect of your social life. It brings steady progress, which boosts the potential around your life. It promotes a lively time of catching up with friends. It brings a leisurely pace that supports renewal and kinship. Events ahead form a favorable window of opportunity for growing your social life.

13 Monday ~ New Moon in Scorpio 09:27, Sun opposed Uranus 17:20

The Sun opposed Uranus transit attracts a restless vibe that gives you the green light to try something new and different. It drives a liberating chapter that offers spontaneity as you get busy expressing your unique individual melody and personality. Opening the book to a new chapter brings a gateway forward. It nurtures your creativity and helps you build something substantial in your life. Life becomes brighter and greener as new possibilities grow in your world.

14 Tuesday

You team up with others who match your interests as you draw movement and discovery into your world. You enter a phase of rising prospects that get the ball rolling on growing your life outwardly. Changing circumstances reinvigorate your life, and from these foundations, you reach for a lofty goal that inspires unique adventures. An inspiring wind carries fresh possibilities around your life. It allows you to pour your energy into enriching your life.

15 Wednesday ~ Mercury sextile Venus 12:47

A loving vibe helps you get past hump day. Today's Mercury sextile Venus adds a positive influence that harmonizes and nurtures well-being in your world. Less stress and more enjoyment grow solid foundations. Personal relationships benefit from open communication leading to fulfillment. Sharing with others adds fuel to your emotional tank. It forms a grounded and stable basis from which to develop your vision.

16 Thursday

Good news lands with a flurry of excitement. It enables you to expand your life and get busy developing a dynamic area that offers room to progress your goals. You will continue to spot opportunities and enjoy life by expanding your talents. You soon get busy planning for future growth in this dynamic landscape filled with possibilities. Life picks up speed and moves towards a faster pace, enabling you to make plans for future growth.

17 Friday ~ Leonids Meteor Shower November 6-30ᵗʰ, Mars trine Neptune 8:36, Sun trine Neptune 14:51

Under the influence of Neptune, creativity soars, epiphany's and lightbulb moments are the order of the day. You find that an area on the back burner for a while gets a shift forward. It sets the growth stage and leads to new adventures that draw excitement and fun. It offers a chance to push back the barriers that limit progress as you get involved in expanding your situation.

18 Saturday ~ Sun conjunct Mars 5:41

Sun conjunct Mars brings abundant energy and initiative, and your drive to try new things increases. A desire for action can cause restlessness if not channeled and released. An area you channel your energy into developing soon returns a positive investment with an influx of inspiration. Working with your talents is a soothing balm that amplifies well-being. The journey brings an expansive chapter of rediscovery and rejuvenation.

19 Sunday

An influx of potential is coming into your social life. It places you in a busy zone where invitations flow into your world, connecting you with lighter energy and a fresh wind possibility. It kicks off a social aspect that brings new adventures into your life. An energizing chapter attracts light-hearted discussions that have you optimistic about future potential. It brings an active environment that improves happiness and harmony in your life.

20 Monday ~ First Quarter Moon in Aquarius 10:50, Sun sextile Pluto 21:26

Today's Sun sextile Pluto transit drives ambitions and sees you heading into the working week with an increased drive to succeed and conquer your goals. Feeling determined and purposeful enables you to nail your tasks quickly and finish work with energy still in the tank. Clearing away limitations and expanding your horizons brings a high note. Improving your circumstances creates a breakthrough that takes you toward a happy chapter.

21 Tuesday

You enter a time of rejuvenation that smooths over the rough edges of your life. It promotes healing and helps you sweep away aspects that are no longer relevant. Moving away from the outworn areas, gently shift your focus towards developing new goals for your life. Setting intentions blends with a mix of manifestation to help open the path ahead. It brings a journey of discovery to the crux of the progression ahead.

22 Wednesday ~ Mars sextile Pluto 1:17, Sun ingress Sagittarius 13:59

Today's transit increases energy in the workplace. No job is too small as you take on the lot and work towards your vision. A lighter, more vibrant environment ahead opens the floodgates to an enterprising time of growth. Getting the chance to branch your talents out and develop new areas brings excitement into your world. Researching options brings a journey that feels healing and rejuvenating.

23 Thursday ~ Thanksgiving Day (USA), Sun square Saturn 9:46

Saturn is the ruler of honoring traditions and following rigid structures that form set boundaries. Today's square illuminates a happy time shared with loved ones, perfect with Saturn, who delights in honoring the past. You invest time and energy in developing an area that enriches your life. It brings a time of chasing dreams and setting goals. Improvement in your home territory becomes a strong focus.

24 Friday ~ Mars ingress Sagittarius 10:10

This transit emits a rebellious vibe that rejuvenates your energy and has you seeking expansion. Spending time with your social set has you feeling valued and appreciated. It brings an active environment that lets the pace and rhythm of life pick up. An offer to mingle is coming up. It starts a social chapter that brings a sense of celebration into your world. It does seem that changes ahead draw new people into your life; it is a time of music, laughter, and conversation.

25 Saturday ~ Mars square Saturn 16:57

Today's aspect can feel challenging as your mind is on Saturn's to-do list. You may find it difficult to relax and unwind when your thoughts turn to the irons you have burning in the fire. Indeed, you are ready to progress in your life and make track of developing your dreams. Listening to your instincts is especially powerful in planning the path. Expanding your life becomes a priority, bringing you in contact with others of a similar mindset.

26 Sunday

An opportunity pops up that feels like a good fit for your life. It brings an active and dynamic environment that lets you accomplish great things. It has a social aspect that offers lively interactions and opportunities to mingle. Getting proactively involved with expanding your social life draws a valuable return. It sees inspiration returning full force. It does bring a friendship that lets you build a stable foundation. It transitions you to a joyful chapter.

27 Monday ~ Beaver Full Moon in Gemini 09:16, Mercury square Neptune 13:26

Today, the Mercury square Neptune aspect can distort or make mountains of molehills. It adds a dash of illusion into your business dealings that can have your head spinning with tall tales and trying to sort the truth from exaggeration. The Full Moon triggers introspection. You can reflect on the past, drawing healing, closure, and transitions into your spirit. It helps you relax and remember as you prepare to turn over a new leaf in your life.

28 Tuesday

Opportunity comes knocking, and this brings a fresh chapter of possibilities. It does let you open pathways of creativity and self-expression. Your ability to nurture a situation draws a boost. It brings a journey that tempts you forward toward expanding your horizons. It brings new people and companions into your world. It's a rewarding time that ushers in thoughtful discussions and enriching dialogues.

29 Wednesday

It's a time of abundance and generosity. It brings a lead worth investigating. You can count your blessings as good fortune flows swiftly into your world. New possibilities arrive that let you forge a trailblazing path forward. The rhythm and pace of your life increase, bringing a social and dynamic chapter. Harmony and abundance surround you and resonate vibrantly.

30 Thursday

You transition towards a new chapter; you leave aspects of the past behind. It creates space to focus your energy on moving forward toward new goals. Changes occur that refine your vision for the path ahead. You invest your time and energy into a situation that brings a valuable phase of growth. A celebration is a cause of excitement and joy. It hits a high note and carries a social environment.

December

Sun	Mon	Tue	Wed	Thu	Fri	Sat
					1	2
3	4	5	6	7	8	9
10	11	12	13	14	15	16
17	18	19	20	21	22	23
24	25	26	27	28	29	30
31						

New Moon

COLD MOON

1 Friday ~ Mercury ingress Capricorn 14:29

Being open to meeting new people promotes a practical sense of connection. It creates space for unique pathways leading to personal growth and companionship. You nurture a social scene that promotes invitations and opportunities to network. Lively discussions with refreshing companions hit a sweet note in your life. It establishes grounded foundations that create a stable basis from which you can grow your world.

2 Saturday ~ Mercury sextile Saturn 15:25

Today's Mercury sextile Saturn transit is favorable for organizing and streamlining your workload to create a stimulating and productive environment. Expressing authority and leadership skills create a purposeful and productive environment. You are likely to receive recognition for the vital work done this year. Something is in the pipeline; a promotion, offer or upgrade. It does open a path forward.

3 Sunday ~ Venus square Pluto 13:29

Today's aspect could see a flare-up of jealousy or possessiveness. Your romantic partner may feel threatened by heightened social activities and invitations pre-run up to Christmas. Take time to support and boost confidence to help offset the Venus square Pluto aspect. Being aware of these fears' dynamics helps keep relationships healthy and balanced.

4 Monday ~ Mercury at Greatest Elongation 21.3 E, Venus ingress Scorpio 18:48

Surprise news leads to a happy occasion. It brings an inspiring journey and offers you room to plot a course forward. Focusing on future goals brings a happy chapter that is undoubtedly more optimistic and joyful. The pace and rhythm of life pick up, let you come out a winner, and this sees a more active and productive environment ahead. More stability and security arrive to bless your romantic life.

5 Tuesday ~ Last Quarter Moon in Virgo 05:50, Venus trine Saturn 22:51

Today's Venus trine Saturn transit is ideal for developing relationships. Self-expression, warmth, and affection flow freely under this favorable aspect. You step out towards growing a journey that speaks to your heart. It is an ideal time to direct your energy toward increasing your social life. Group activities ahead bring news and excitement to the forefront as it opens a door forward in your life. It helps you achieve a golden phase of improving your circumstances.

6 Wednesday ~ Neptune turns direct in Pisces, 12:38

With Neptune turning direct in Pisces, an extra emotional element adds flavor to your dreams, creativity, and vision. Wistful thinking, goals, and fantasies let you move beyond the material world and escape into fanciful thoughts about future possibilities. Research ahead brings a passageway towards growth. You move towards developing an endeavor that enhances your abilities and deepens your knowledge. Working with your creative ideas brings rising prospects.

7 Thursday ~ Hanukkah (begins at sunset)

You will likely be busy for the next few weeks, especially with communication as news arrives. It does trigger a social atmosphere; you'll gain a sense of belonging from connecting with friends. It does boost the areas of your life that are currently quiet. Finding a way to channel your energy into positive outlets brings a pleasing result. It does nurture a happy time in your life.

8 Friday ~ Mercury trine Jupiter 4:04

Mercury's trine Jupiter transit today attracts a rich landscape of potential that sees your luck rising under sunny skies. Your life heads to an upswing soon. It brings the right conditions to expand your social life and nurture companionship. A positive influence raises confidence and brings invitations to head out with friends. There is much to look forward to as it marks the start of a refreshing time that lights up pathways that nurture social engagement.

9 Saturday

Life brings a trailblazing journey that offers a whirlwind of activity in your social life. It connects you with unique characters who add zest to your life. Mingling with friends brings expansion and growth into focus. Blossoming potential swirls around the periphery of your situation but soon grows into a valid path forward. You open a compelling way that brings magic into your life.

10 Sunday ~ Venus opposed Jupiter 3:34

This astrological transit adds an indulgent vibration and has you wanting to explore hedonism, romance, and magic. Pursuing pleasure attracts social engagement, relaxation, and unwinding with a leisurely influence restoring well-being. Riding a wave of hopeful energy, you shift your focus to exploring the possibilities. A lighter vibration brings exciting adventures along the way.

11 Monday ~ Mercury sextile Venus 19:22

Communication flows freely into your social life, attracting invitations and mingling opportunities. The Mercury sextile Venus aspect nurtures stable foundations and happiness. It brings a productive landscape into view, attracting rising prospects and creating a breezy time shared with friends. A positive influence adds fuel to creativity, and the sharing of ideas charts an auspicious journey towards fresh possibilities.

12 Tuesday ~ New Moon in Sagittarius 23:32

Engaging with a broader world of potential sees companionship flourish as new ideas and possibilities crop up. You meet a progressive person who helps you step into a different landscape. It brings a motivational time of investing energy into your social life. Lively discussions ensure bright ideas grow your creativity and bring new projects and endeavors to the surface.

13 Wednesday ~ Mercury turns Retrograde in Capricorn 7:08
Geminids Meteor Shower Dec 7-17th

Mercury turns retrograde, seeing communication issues cropping up over the next few weeks. Plans and times quickly become mixed as messages scramble during this more chaotic planetary phase. Shaking off the heavy vibrations releases stress. Being selective about who you let into your inner circle will draw positive results for your social life. Associate with those who uplift your spirit and nurture your world.

14 Thursday

Your thoughts turn to the past and the precious memories you keep close to your heart. It does bring a time of sentimental looking back and understanding more profound messages around your life. A time of healing and renewal opens the door to a new phase of growing your life. Stepping back enables you to focus on your priorities without distraction. It creates space to nurture your soul and draw rejuvenation and balance into your surroundings.

15 Friday ~ Hanukkah (ends at sunset)

A focus on social engagement opens a path of connection and companionship. It brings a positive influence that helps you grow a meaningful journey forward. It brings a more comprehensive theme of change and expansion into your life. Socialising and networking lead to a lovely get-together with like-minded people who boost morale and share ideas. It brings a spontaneous and lively environment to enjoy.

16 Saturday

A golden aspect weaves through your life this holiday season. It brings a treasured time that offers ample opportunity to connect with your friends and loved ones. The good news is coming; something is on offer that takes your talents to a new level. It amplifies your potential. It brings a remarkable shift that allows you to pursue goals and build your foundations successfully.

17 Sunday

It is a time of surprise communication and messages. The news arrives that offers a social aspect. Something comes up, an invitation, and you dive into a new journey on the spur of the moment. It is an enchanting chapter that brings a quickening of pace. It opens new possibilities. A situation you invest your energy into holds water and soon blossoms into a meaningful area that inspires your mind.

18 Monday ~ Mercury trine Jupiter 14:33

Mercury trine Jupiter transit brings optimism, luck, and good news. Information arrives that bodes well for your social life. Indeed, it's easy to make new friends under this favorable influence that sparks social engagement and thoughtful discussions with friendly characters. A friendship blossoms and brings a lively chapter into your life that offers expansion.

19 Tuesday ~ First Quarter Moon in Pisces 18:39

Increasing opportunities visit your life to tempt you forward. It is a compelling call to action. A strong emphasis on improving your world launches a chapter of growth. It brings an exciting opportunity that connects to your social life. Luck is on your side; it brings opportunities to mingle and connect with your broader friends. You also attract a new person into your life who has experience and wisdom to share.

20 Wednesday

A social aspect lights the path forward. Refreshing options are imminent that bring friends and colleagues together. It washes away the stress and outworn energy. Mingling and networking create space to draw your friends closer. Connecting with your broader social environment draws dividends. It places you in the box seat to improve your life by sharing thoughts and ideas with other trailblazers.

21 Thursday ~ Ursids Meteor Shower Dec 17ᵗʰ – 25ᵗʰ, Venus opposed Uranus 7:04, Mercury sextile Saturn 12:35

Today's Venus opposed Uranus alignment brings growth to personal relationships. Increasing synergy and chemistry could spark a new romance or flirtation opportunity. It ignites new energy that kicks off an exciting chapter in your social life. It brings a stunning chapter of magic and mayhem. It creates space for a fresh chapter; it washes away the stress and nourishes your soul.

**22 Friday ~ Sun ingress Capricorn 3:24, Yule/Winter Solstice 03:28,
Sun conjunct Mercury 18:53**

The Sun conjunct Mercury aspect favors communication. It brings the sharing of thoughtful dialogues and entertaining discussions. A fresh wind of possibility soon breezes into your life to open a new chapter. It leads to an interesting social aspect that feeds your soul. It sees you spending more time with those who connect well with your take on life.

23 Saturday ~ Mercury ingress Sagittarius 6:19

A group environment triggers options for collaboration. Your situation is evolving, bringing expansion as you cultivate your talents and expand your reach into new areas. It brings a time of rising prospects which offers a chance to build your dreams and develop your goals. It brings a vibrant atmosphere that connects you with kindred spirits. It has you feeling cheerful about engaging in a group environment.

24 Sunday ~ Sun sextile Saturn 17:28

Sun sextile Saturn transit lends patience to family gatherings, which can be a godsend if your family dynamics are challenging. You may need some downtime to process sensitive emotions. If the past keeps cropping up in your mind, it's a sign to pause and reflect on your life's journey. Relaxing in a calming, ambient environment helps untangle knots and weave a firm and balanced foundation.

25 Monday ~ Christmas Day, Venus trine Neptune 17:15

Venus trine Neptune transit is the perfect backdrop to Christmas. It attracts creativity, well-being, and fulfillment. This transit favors singing, music, and delight in the day's celebration. Connecting with your tribe, you relish diving into refreshing conversations as you enjoy a more meaningful sense of bonding with friends and family. Being with people who resonate on your wavelength nurtures a happy environment.

26 Tuesday ~ Kwanzaa begins

A person reaches out to share news about a community event. It does lead to an invitation out and about. It connects you with the right opportunity to improve your social life. It translates into a journey that offers room for progression. Artful communication follows with an admirer. It brings a fruitful chapter that draws a sense of connection with someone who triggers your interest.

27 Wednesday ~ Cold Full Moon, Moon before Yule in Cancer 0:34, Mercury square Neptune 7:36, Sun trine Jupiter 15:28

The Sun trine Jupiter aspect lights up good fortune across the board. New possibilities blossom as a favorable wind ignites your passion and imagination. The Full Moon promotes a time of reflection and introspection. Your life has undergone some rapid changes, and taking time to process your changing emotional landscape helps nurture well-being and harmony.

28 Thursday ~ Mercury conjunct Mars 0:26, Mars square Neptune 22:15

The Mars square Neptune aspect brings gossip and scandal to your ears. You hear surprising news that feels disconcerting. Suppose something doesn't ring true to your ears. In that case, you should do your own investigating as this transit could draw misinformation leading to confusion. It delivers a message about finding the truth. If troubled by recent events, know that you can draw balance into your life by slowing down and exploring growth pathways. It gives you a leg up on creating an environment that brings stability into focus.

29 Friday ~ Venus sextile Pluto 6:00, Venus ingress Sagittarius 20:21

The Venus sextile Pluto transit deepens romantic love and grows relationship potential. It brings an expressive time of nurturing a wellspring of abundance in your world. News ahead brings a dream into focus. It gets you in touch with meaningful areas that inspire your spirit and improve stability in your world. It brings soul food in the form of creative possibilities that gently let inspiration flow into your world.

30 Saturday

Information arrives, which opens the door to a fresh start. Notable changes attract growth and progression. It encourages you to pour time and energy into developing your social life. As you blaze a trail towards an engaging atmosphere that nurtures a self-expressive and confident vibe, you enjoy a refreshing change of pace that offers expansion. It helps you find your groove as life expands outwardly with friends and companions.

31 Sunday ~ New Year's Eve, Jupiter turns direct in Taurus at 2:41

In a promising sign, Jupiter turns direct on New Year's Eve. It foretells bright blessings, good fortune, and opportunities on the horizon. Unlimited possibilities spark inspiration and wonder. The power of your intention nurtures creativity. It brings progression to the forefront of your life. It draws a new chapter that helps you get busy making plans and developing a project close to your heart.

Mystic Cat

Printed in Great Britain
by Amazon

14214315R00102